D1583323

The Flower in Season

THE
FLOWER IN
SEASON

A CALENDAR OF
WILD FLOWERS

Jocelyn Brooke

WITH ILLUSTRATIONS BY
Charles W. Stewart

London
THE BODLEY HEAD

First published 1952

Printed in Great Britain by
UNWIN BROTHERS LIMITED, WOKING AND LONDON
for JOHN LANE THE BODLEY HEAD LIMITED
28 Little Russell St., London, W.C.1

TO

Desmond MacCarthy

IN HOMAGE AND
AFFECTION

Contents

AUTHOR'S NOTE—Page 9

FOREWORD—Page 11

JANUARY—Page 15

FEBRUARY—Page 28

MARCH—Page 38

APRIL—Page 54

MAY—Page 71

JUNE—Page 86

JULY—Page 110

AUGUST—Page 123

SEPTEMBER—Page 136

OCTOBER—Page 144

NOVEMBER—Page 152

DECEMBER—Page 155

List of Illustrations

FRONTISPIECE
Helleborus foetidus

JANUARY—Page 17
Petasites fragrans   Snowdrop
Winter Aconite   Leaves of Cuckoo-pint

FEBRUARY—Page 29
Butcher's Broom   Helleborus viridis
Daphne mezereum

MARCH—Page 39
Daffodil   Celandine
Windflower (Anemone nemorosa)   Blackthorn

APRIL—Page 55
Primrose   Bluebell
Early Purple Orchid   Fritillary (Fritillaria meleagris)
Pasque Flower (Anemone pulsatilla)   Moschatel
Cowslip

MAY—Page 73
Columbine   Red Campion
Early Spider Orchid (Ophrys aranifera)   Lady Orchid
Yellow Archangel   Stitchwort

JUNE—Page 87
Corn Poppy   Fumitory
Bee Orchid   Bladder Campion
Ox-eye Daisy

JULY—Page 111
Centaury   Great Knapweed
Rest-harrow   Pyramidal Orchid
Scabious

AUGUST—Page 125
Sea Holly   Horned Poppy

SEPTEMBER—Page 137
Hop

OCTOBER—Page 145
Ivy   Spindleberries

NOVEMBER—Page 153
Wild Clematis (Old Man's Beard)

DECEMBER—Page 157
Holly   Mistletoe

Author's Note

I WISH to express my gratitude to the numerous kind friends who, by their help and encouragement, have assisted in the making of this book. I am especially grateful to Sir Desmond MacCarthy for his great kindness in looking at the proofs, and for some valuable suggestions; also to Richard Chopping and Dennis Wirth-Miller for a pleasant week-end spent in ransacking their botanical library; and to Jonathan Curling, who first suggested that the book should be written.

My acknowledgments are also due to the following, for their kind permission to reproduce copyright material:

Messrs. Faber and Faber (for extracts from poems by T. S. Eliot, W. H. Auden and Louis MacNeice); Mrs. Edward Thomas and Messrs. Faber and Faber (for extracts from the *Collected Poems* of Edward Thomas); Mr. Walter de la Mare and Messrs. Faber and Faber (for an extract from the *Collected Poems* of Walter de la Mare); Mrs. Frieda Lawrence and Messrs. William Heinemann (for the lines from *Sicilian Cyclamens*, included in the *Poems* of D. H. Lawrence); The Society of Authors (as Literary Representatives of the Trustees of the Estate of the late A. E. Housman) and Messrs. Jonathan Cape (for extracts from the *Collected Poems* of A. E. Housman); the Oxford University Press (for extracts from the poems of Gerard Manley Hopkins); Messrs. Chatto and Windus (for quotations from *Swann's Way* by Marcel Proust, translated by C. K. Scott-Moncrieff); Mrs. W. B. Yeats and Messrs. Macmillan (for an extract from the *Collected Poems* of W. B. Yeats); Messrs. Macmillan (for quotations from *The Golden Bough* by Sir James Frazer); Sir Francis Meynell and Messrs. Hollis and Carter (for the lines from Francis Thompson's *The Poppy*).

. . . and pull the flower in season,
  Before desire shall fail.

A. E. HOUSMAN

Foreword

IT is best to begin by saying what this book is not: it is neither an anthology, an autobiography nor (let me hasten to add) a botanical textbook. It is merely a book about wild flowers for those who like wild flowers—I am preaching, in fact, to the converted, and in writing it I have addressed myself chiefly to those who, like myself, are not so much botanists as botanophils.

It is also a book about the months: I have always been a month-addict, and am still. In childhood, the names of the months had for me a special and very potent poetry of their own, and the calendar seemed no mere artificial, man-made affair, but a true reflection of the order of nature. The months (with their names) had been, as I supposed, instituted like the rest of the world on the First Day—which I very naturally assumed to have been the First of January; and the special imagery which I attached to these fixed, immutable divisions of the year was, from my earliest days, largely concerned with flowers. Thus the wild-sounding, masculine, adventurous concept of "March" was symbolized inevitably, for me, by the Coltsfoot; while the milder, more feminine, rather melancholy personality of "April" was incarnated (rather unsuitably, as it happens) in the Early Purple Orchis. Sometimes a particular month would be thus linked with a flower which I myself had not actually found, but which had appealed especially to my imagination: August, for instance, was coloured for me with the dull, purpureal splendour of Purple Loosestrife, which didn't happen to grow near my home, but with which I was familiar from Edward Step's *Wayside and Woodland Blossoms*, in which the flowering season was given as "July to September."

To this day, such associations retain for me much of their old potency; and I can scarcely encounter, even in the most banal circumstances (a bank statement or a newspaper report), the mere names of the months, without a faint stirring of memory, a sudden fleeting vision of the flowers which, in childhood, were linked for me, indissolubly, with those magical and resounding syllables.

But the lunar calendar is, for the botanist, an unsatisfactory and arbitrary conception: too many plants have the disobliging habit of refusing to fit into it. The floras may state, glibly, that the flowering season of *Primula vulgaris* (for instance) is "from April to May"; yet most of us have picked primroses in February, and stray specimens can usually be found, with any luck, at Christmas time—or, for that matter, in August or September. Moreover, the flowering seasons of plants vary enormously according to climate and altitude: a meadow-growing plant, for instance, which flowers normally in June will, if it happens to have strayed into the high mountain pastures, postpone its appearance for a month or more. And an abnormally mild season always produces its anomalies: a fairly recent instance was the astonishing spring of 1945, when bluebells and purple orchids could be gathered in the woods in mid-March.

Yet despite their frequent unpunctuality, flowers continue to be associated, for most people, with particular months. Think of any month in the year and, ten to one, if you have even the faintest, most unprofessional interest in botany, you will immediately think of a corresponding flower. The mere man-in-the-street (that convenient abstraction) can hardly fail to connect April with primroses or June with roses; and such associations have, I suppose, taken deeper root in England than elsewhere, for we are, after all, a nation of flower-lovers. It is one of our more engaging national traits, and is reflected in our poetry, where, from Chaucer onwards, the references to flowers must far outnumber those to be found in the literature of any other country.

I have said that this book is not an anthology; but it is, I'm afraid, like *Hamlet*, "full of quotations." Botanophils have a bad habit of quoting "bits" about their favourites, and I am no exception; the reason, I think, is that one feels impelled to justify one's fondness for a particular plant by quoting the praises of other and more eminent writers. No scholar myself, I cannot compete with the erudite botanographers; and I shall be duly rebuked, no doubt, by my fellow-botanophils for my omissions. I have consulted (let me be quite frank) no recondite works merely for the sake of digging out curious quotations; I have used, merely, such books as I happen to possess or be familiar with: Gerarde and Culpepper are two of my favourites, and I confess to an incurable weakness for Victorian lady-botanists such as Miss Pratt, Miss Plues and Mrs. Lankester.

I shall be castigated too, no doubt, for my omissions among the flowers themselves. But if I am accused of favouritism, I can only admit as gracefully as possible, that the charge is justified. One can't possibly include, in a book of this kind, more than a fraction of the plants in the British Flora. I know that the reader will lament the absence of his special favourites—"How *could* you leave out the Cheddar Pink (or Spring Gentian or Globe-flower)?" I can only answer that this is *my* book, after all, and that I have my favourites too. Moreover, I am a Southerner, and I have a penchant for the chalk-down flora, particularly the orchids; I know little about the Alpines; I am frankly bored by certain Natural Orders—the Grasses, for instance, and the Goosefoots; and though I am fond of fungi, I cannot be bothered with bryophytes.

One word more: I have tried, so far as possible, not to "cheat"—to include, for instance, under "March" a plant which, except in very exceptional circumstances, can't be found till May. It is a temptation rather hard to resist, for flowers, as I've said, are often unpunctual, and one does derive a particular thrill from coming upon a plant out of season: it seems, at the time, like a personal triumph, and one develops a kind of proprietary interest in one's discovery. I have found that even quite serious botanists are not immune from this peculiar (if harmless) form of snobbery: "You wouldn't believe it, but I found *Ophrys aranifera* on April 5th this year." "That's nothing, my dear fellow, in 1945 I found it on March 29th."

I have tried to be honest in this respect, and to be as accurate as possible in other matters; I am not, however, a professional botanist, and I have written this book (let me repeat the warning) for people who, like myself, are merely "fond" of flowers, unscientifically and for their own sake.

13

January

JANUARY, the Janus-faced guardian of the door, looking forward and backward: the syllable "Jan" is cold and frozen, unbending on "uary" into a warmer, more flexile sound; a cold, white month, its candour tinged only faintly with the precocious gold of Jasmine and the Winter Aconite. . . . But the word, if cold, seems clear and sunlit by contrast with the dank, heavy, ashen-grey syllables of "December": and is it merely this association that makes one think that there is, in fact, a tendency for the first days of the year to be bright and frosty?

As I write, on New Year's Eve, the weather seems to have become suddenly "January" weather, after a spell of grey, muggy days following Christmas. In childhood, I was sure that the weather changed in this way on New Year's Day; and I was pretty certain that, if I went into the garden, I should see the first "bulbs" piercing the glacial earth with their green spears. . . . And in fact, if it doesn't happen quite overnight, there is, in a fairly mild season, a perceptible quickening of life between Christmas and Twelfth Night: the bulbous plants really do begin to appear, if they haven't done so already, and one notices the swelling chorus of bird-song at morning and evening.

January is a woodland month: one must search the sheltered places for the first flowers—and not only the woods, but high, thickset hedgerows, and banks screened from the north wind, at the hill's foot, or beneath the sea-cliffs. My own type-flower for January is the Winter Heliotrope, *Petasites fragrans*, described by the floras, rather superciliously, as an "alien," but long naturalized in the south, and particularly in sheltered places by the sea. It is a Butterbur, a small edition of the big, native Butterbur which is sometimes abundant by streamsides in March and April. Winter Heliotrope, unlike its British cousin, has a delicious scent; and its pale, pinkish-white clusters are not out of place in the garden though, once established, it spreads like a weed. Gardeners should keep a wary eye on this "alien": as an immigrant, it is apt to abuse one's hospitality—and even in the wild state, it will cover whole acres in the space of a few years. (I remember, as a child, being delighted to find a small patch of it at Sandgate, on the side of a path near a garden; it has now become a common weed in the neighbourhood.)

Two other aliens—or "doubtful natives"—belong to January: Snowdrop and Winter Aconite. About the Snowdrop, botanists seem still unwilling to make up their minds: "probably not indigenous," say Bentham and Hooker, though it has been naturalized so long that one might have supposed it would have acquired British citizenship by this time. None the less, the Snowdrop, unlike the Winter Heliotrope (a far more recent immigrant) seems always, when one finds it, something of a foreigner. It is easily propagated, and, where it becomes well established, is extremely abundant: in parks and plantations in many parts of the country it covers the ground in great drifts of whiteness, like a heavy hoar frost. Yet it strays but seldom into the real woods— and then only into well fenced and carefully preserved ones. This preference for privacy seems to argue a certain lack of enterprise; the Snowdrop ought to have become a common wild flower, but it has remained—*as* a wild flower—a rarity. One name for it, by the way, is Candlemas-bells, and it is the flower associated, suitably enough, with the Purification of the Blessed Virgin Mary.

Winter Aconite, too, remains a rarity in the wild state, though Gerarde, writing at the end of the sixteenth century, remarks that "we have great quantitie of it in our London gardens," adding that it was reported "to prevaile mightily against the biting of scorpions, and is of such force, that if the scorpion passe by where it groweth and touch the same, presently he becommeth dull, heavie, and senceless, and if the same scorpion by chance touch the White Hellebor, is presently delivered from his drowsines." One has never heard that Elizabethan London was plagued by scorpions, but if the scorpions were there, so

was the Aconite—or Winter Wolfsbane, as Gerarde calls it, by association with the true Wolfsbane, or Monkshood, which is also the true Aconite, *Aconitum napellus* (Winter Aconite, *Eranthis hyemalis*, is not really an aconite at all). With its trim green ruff it is truly a Tudor flower, and it may well have seemed patriotic to grow it in one's garden, as doubtless Gerarde did in Holborn. Like the Snowdrop, it is exceedingly abundant in plantations and private woodlands, but even less often makes its escape into the wild. I remember, one winter in Italy, during the war, coming upon it in a hedgerow; it was a grey, January afternoon, and the countryside looked very English: I looked at the Aconite suspiciously—doubtless an "escape from cultivation," I thought (there was, in fact, a village nearby). Suddenly I realized that I was, after all, not in England, but in Italy—the Aconite was truly wild!

This problem of plant "naturalization" gives much trouble to botanists, and offers unrivalled opportunities to the pedant. How long must a plant be "naturalized" before it becomes a "native"? There are those who would tell us that the common Corn Poppy is not a true native—a manifest absurdity; one might as well (and perhaps with more reason) say that the Royal Family is not English. The Pheasant's Eye, too (*Adonis annua*)—another scarlet-flowered haunter of corn-fields—is usually marked with an asterisk, in the floras, as an "introduced species": yet it is as wild as the poppy, though rare. An orchid, *Gymnadenia odoratissima*, which has made sporadic appearances up and down the country for a century or more, is not mentioned in the floras at all. Why? It is, I suppose, regarded by botanists as an *arriviste*, not worthy of recognition until its dubious origins have been conveniently forgotten. . . . The Aconite is a borderline case: it has been with us for at least three hundred years, but (like the Snowdrop) it has tended to confine itself to plantations, and is still regarded as a foreigner. Winter Heliotrope, on the other hand, though introduced only a hundred and fifty years ago, has become in many districts a wayside weed: it practically "counts" as indigenous, nowadays, and will doubtless receive, in due course, official recognition.

This, in fact, seems to be the ultimate test: if a plant becomes a "weed," one is almost bound to admit it into the British Flora. (Another example is *Lepidium draba*, a pest in the southern counties, and not even beautiful, but still officially liable to be convicted under the botanical equivalent of 18B.)

Aconites, those prim little Tudor courtiers, may not be admitted as true natives by the botanical purist; but nobody, so far as I know, has ever cast any doubts on the Dandelion's claim to be a true Briton. Golden as the Aconite, a handsome plebeian, *Taraxacum officinale* would be more popular (especially among gardeners) if it were rarer. Perhaps I shouldn't include it under this month—it doesn't really achieve its full glory till March—but January is not so well provided with flowers that one can afford to neglect even a plant which, as Culpepper remarks, is "vulgarly called Piss-a-Beds." And the Dandelion, as Culpepper adds, "flowereth in one Place or other almost all the Year long," a habit which it shares with the Gorse, *Ulex europæus*, which may also be justifiably classified as a January flower.

In England, the Dandelion is treated with a contempt which it hardly deserves—a point which didn't escape Culpepper who, after listing its numerous "virtues" (it was good for "Gall, Spleen, Jaundice, Hypochondriacal Melancholy, Dysury, Consumption, Cachexia, Watching, Heat, Agues, Pestilence") adds the following little homily:

"You see here what Virtues this common Herb hath, and that's the Reason the *French* and *Dutch* so often eat them in the Spring; and now, if you look a little farther, you may see plainly, without a Pair of Spectacles, that Foreign Physicians are not so selfish as ours are, but more communicative of the Virtues of Plants to People."

Whatever one may think of the "selfish" attitude of English physicians, the fact remains that we are not a nation of salad-eaters: we like our lettuces in the summer months, but our winter salads are practically all imported, and seldom obtainable at the ordinary small-town greengrocer, who will tell you that he has "no demand" for such outlandish foreign stuff as endive or chicory. Such being the case, the Dandelion (closely allied to the chicory group) is unlikely to

become popular; yet its leaves, when blanched, are not inferior to those
of the curly endive, and are good even in the green state, if one can
find them young enough. There are, too, a number of ways of cooking
them, though the fact that writers of cookery-books (such as the
excellent one by Boulestin) so often refer to the plant as *pissenlit*, may
have discouraged the British housewife from attempting a Dandelion
soup.

Another all-the-year-round flower which, like the Dandelion, is
often coyly described in botany books as a "humble weed," is the
Red Deadnettle. Later in the year, one is apt to pass it over; but in
January one appreciates the whorls of small, purple, labiate flowers
shaded by the dull-green leaves which, if you squeeze them, have a
faintly aromatic, rather "cottagey" smell. The flowers, according to
Gerarde, can be "baked with sugar as roses are . . . which is used to
make the hart merrie; to make a good colour in the face, and to make
the vitall spirits more fresh and lively." One can hardly imagine anybody taking the trouble to gather enough Deadnettle flowers to be
worth "baking with sugar"; but to find the quiet, undistinguished
little plant in full bloom under the January hedgerows is enough in
itself to "make the hart merrie."

Apart from its use in confectionery, it had a reputation for "taking
away wens and hard swellings, the King's evill, inflammation of the
kernels under the eares and jawes," and various other complaints.
According to Anne Pratt, it was at one time used in "pottage," along
with borage, avens, violets and a number of other improbable herbs.
"We fear," adds Miss Pratt cautiously, "that few modern palates
would be gratified by the preparation."

Along with the Deadnettle, one can group a few more all-the-year-
rounders—Groundsel, Chickweed and "the emperice, the floure of
floures alle," as Chaucer called it: *Bellis perennis*, the Common Daisy.
One may even come across a January buttercup—it will usually be
Ranunculus bulbosus, easy to identify by the turned-down sepals.

But January, as I have said, is a woodland month: and in the clear,
frosty days, among the bare trees, one will be constantly titillated by

deceptive gleams of verdure—the leaves of honeysuckle, for instance, a deciduous plant which almost deserves to be called an evergreen, for there is no month in the year when it is entirely bare of foliage. Honeysuckle, however, will not oblige us by *flowering* in January—any more than the Cuckoo-pint or Lords-and-ladies, another plant whose leaves are a delight in themselves: glossy, bright-green spears piercing the woodland beech-mast, or lighting like sudden barium flames the sheltered hedgerow. Cuckoo-pint leaves have an edible, appetizing look—they ought to make a good salad, but are in fact poisonous, though the plant is not quite without "virtues," since a substance called "Portland sago" is (or used to be) made from the dried root.

After a mild December, the woods and hedgerows offer a surprising display of young green: as I write, on New Year's Day, the hedges are already full of the feathery, fern-like foliage of Beaked Parsley (*Anthriscus sylvestris*)—the commonest but not the least charming of a rather dull family. Like the Deadnettle, Beaked Parsley is said to be edible—though Anne Pratt, always enterprising in culinary matters, is not encouraging, referring to it merely as "wholesome," and adding that, though the leaves are "eaten in some parts of the kingdom," the roots are poisonous and, "when they have been eaten as parsnips, have in some cases proved fatal."

Anthriscus is a surprisingly hardy plant, considering its unsubstantial, feathery appearance; so, too, is *Adoxa moschatellina*, the Moschatel, which is usually showing in the woods before the end of the month, and may even be in flower. It is one of the most delicate and vulnerable-looking of our native plants, and its graceful growth demands, one feels, a handsomer flower; yet the little green clock-towers are pretty enough in a subdued way.

The leaves of Bugle are showing too: thick, compact tufts close to the ground, beautifully tinged with mauve and brownish-crimson, carrying a hint, already, of the four-square turrets of dull blue which will appear in late April or early May. In sheltered places on this New Year's Day one could detect the first, barbed shoots of Dog's Mercury—

a dull plant, but so inseparable from one's idea of a wood that it acquires, by association, a somewhat spurious charm. By the end of the month it can usually be found in bloom—though the flowers are even less spectacular than those of Moschatel. Its cousin, Annual Mercury, is already—or still—in flower in the garden, another all-the-year-rounder, of which I cannot bring myself to say a single good word: it is just a weed, though according to Culpepper it is useful to the gynæcologist. "*Mercury*, they say, owns the Herb," he remarks, deferring to received opinion, "but I rather think it is *Venus* . . . for I never heard that *Mercury* ever minded Women's Business so much. . . ."

On this same New Year's Day on which I write, I was more interested to see the first green shoot of an orchid—*Orchis purpurea*, the Lady Orchid—just visible above the beech-mast in a copse near my home. I do not remember noticing these leaves much before March in previous years: orchids vary a good deal in their seasons of growth, and the Lady certainly exerts a woman's privilege, sometimes proving irritatingly unpunctual in her appearances.

It was cheering to see signs, already, of this most magnificent of British Orchids: I shall have something more to say on the subject in June. Meanwhile, I must add that the Lady is my local celebrity—a very local one, not to be found outside Kent, in which county I happen to live. Less local, but not especially common, is the Guelder Rose, whose scarlet berries are still lingering not far away from the orchid. The autumn berries this year are, in fact, unusually persistent—spindle, rose-hips and black bryony can still be seen in some quantity, lingering on in the hedgerows where, already, the hazel catkins are lengthening, and taking on a faintly green or sulphurous tinge. The dogwood saplings, too, seem to have deepened in colour in the last week or two: in to-day's sunlight, they are flushed to a rich, clear claret colour—a shade which is rather rare in the plant world, the only other example I can think of, off-hand, being a rare orchid, *Epipactis rubiginosa*, confined to North Wales and one or two counties in northern England.

I have left till last the grandest of January flowers—*Helleborus foetidus*, the Stinking Hellebore, Bearsfoot, Setterwort or (as it should be called) the English Christmas Rose. It is a woodland plant, and a rarity—preferring chalk and limestone, and confined to southern England, where it has a habit of frequenting the neighbourhood of ruined abbeys. It was anciently much cultivated as a medicinal herb, and, like the Aconite and Snowdrop, it is sometimes viewed with a certain suspicion by botanists. Yet I have found it, in the Cotswolds, far from any human habitation, and it seems genuinely wild, too, in some parts of Kent.

The Hellebore is one of those plants which are continuously beautiful: the handsome, much-divided leaves are evergreen, and are disposed with a charming symmetry about the tough, upright stems. From the dark mass of foliage springs, in December, the tall panicle of flower-buds—pale, whitish-green, contrasting oddly with the leaves' iron darkness. The flowers expand slowly—pale green Christmas Roses, fringed with dull purple. I am not "cheating" when I call the Hellebore a January flower; but its flowering season is variable, and in a hard winter it may not be out till February. Gilbert White, however, records it for January 2nd, and mentions it in a letter as one of the "more rare" plants of his acquaintance:

"*Helleborus foetidus* . . . all over the High-wood and Coney-croft-hanger: this continues a great branching plant the winter through, blossoming about January, and is very ornamental in shady walks and shrubberies. The good women give the leaves powdered to children troubled with worms; but it is a violent remedy, and ought to be administered with caution."

So indeed it ought: all the Hellebores are poisonous, and the Setterwort is not the least deadly. "Twenty grains taken inwardly," says Culpepper, "is a sufficient dose," and one can quite believe it. Gerarde, writing nearly two hundred years before Gilbert White, also refers to Setterwort as a vermifuge: "the leaves . . . dried in an oven after the bread is drawne out, and the powder thereof taken in a figge or raison, or strained upon a peece of bread spred with honie and eaten, killeth wormes in children exceedingly." The name "Setterwort," he adds, refers to the use of the plant as a cure for diseases of cattle: "they cut a slit or hole in the dewlap as they terme it (which is an emptie skin under the throte of the beast) wherein they put a peece of the roote . . . suffering it there to remaine for certaine daies togither; which manner of curing they do call settering of their cattell. . . ."

This seems a plausible enough derivation; yet I have heard of modern attempts to derive the name from "Satyr-wort," on what conceivable grounds I cannot imagine.

Gerarde allows the Setterwort to be a wild plant, though noting that it was prevalent "in our London gardens." Anne Pratt, however, three hundred years later, observes that it is "rarely, if ever, truly wild." The powdered roots, she adds, mixed with meal, "are said to destroy mice." She quotes too, a little poem by Bishop Mant:

> Within the moist and shady glade
> What plant, in suit of green array'd,
> All heedless of the winter cold,
> Inhabits! Foremost to unfold
> Though half-conceal'd, its bloom globose,
> Whose petals green, o'er-lapp'd, and close,
> Present each arch'd converging lip,
> Embroider'd with a purple tip;
> And green its floral leaves expand,
> With fingers like a mermaid's hand.

Not very distinguished, perhaps—but that "mermaid's hand" is a pleasant conceit; it seems meaningless, unless one knows the plant, and I had to think, myself, for some moments, before I saw the Bishop's point. The leaflets growing in the axils of the flowering stems are, in fact, very curiously shaped—palmate, pale green, with a somewhat fin-like appearance. The Bishop may not have been much of a poet, but he was, one feels, an observant and accurate botanist. Miss Pratt quotes extensively from his work (her books are full of quotations from forgotten poets); but I have never, so far as I can remember, come across him elsewhere but in her pages. Presumably he was that same Richard Mant, Bishop of Down, Connor and Dromore (1776–1848), the list of whose publications occupies no less than five pages in the British Museum Catalogue, and includes, among other, lesser items, a monumental *History of the Church of Ireland*. He seems ripe for "revival"—lesser men than he have been disinterred, in recent years, for the amusement (if not for the edification) of a later generation.

Miss Pratt herself, for that matter, lacks a biographer—and her own works have all been long out of print. Most entertaining of Victorian lady botanists, she is surely worth reprinting, if only in an abridged edition, with a short memoir. . . . The memoir, I think, would necessarily be brief: for hers was not an eventful life. From internal evidence, I had always pictured her as tough, tweeded and immensely energetic, and once, in a book of mine, wrote a short sketch of her in this character. Later, mistrusting such speculative methods, I looked her up in the *Dictionary of National Biography*, and found that, far from being the strapping dame I had imagined, she was in fact a life-long invalid; it was an elder sister, I learnt, who had collected most of the plants which Miss Pratt so sensitively described and illustrated. So much for the "intuitive approach."

Born in 1806, at Strood, Kent, Miss Pratt later settled at Dover, and, at the ripe age of sixty (and in spite of being an invalid), married a Mr. Pearless of East Grinstead—an occurrence which seems to have benefited her health, for she survived thereafter for a further twenty-seven years, dying in 1893 at the age of eighty-seven.

Like her favourite Bishop Mant, she was a prolific and most industrious writer, and her *magnum opus*, *Flowering Plants, Grasses and Ferns of Great Britain*, is still an excellent bedside-book, though a little out-of-date as a handbook of field botany. Diffuse, erudite, pious but almost never dull, Anne Pratt is really (though she aspired to be up-to-date and "scientific") in the tradition of the seventeenth-century herbalists: there is the same prodigality in her work, she was not content, one feels, merely to *describe* a plant, she believed in collecting all the available information about it, however recondite. Her book, in consequence, is a fascinating compendium of history, gastronomy, folklore and a dozen other subjects connected, however remotely, with plants. She reminds one, indeed, not so much of Gerarde as of Burton's *Anatomy*: botany, one feels, was for Miss Pratt what "Melancholy" was to Burton—largely an excuse for writing at considerable length about the things which interested her. It is a literary *genre* which, in an age of specialists, has become rather unfashionable; myself, I am inclined to regret its passing, and should like to see it revived.

I have divagated, unpardonably, from the Hellebore, but it is a suggestive and evocative plant, and for me is peculiarly rich in associations. Long before I found it in England, I saw it in the woods above Montreux and Vevey, where it is extremely abundant. When I returned to school in England (I was at Bedales at the time) I shocked Geoffrey Crump, the English master, by writing a poem about it—in *vers libres* (which was not, in those days, considered a suitable medium for schoolboys). I hope he has since forgiven me for this lapse. . . . As I write, the Hellebore is coming into flower in my garden, where it has flourished for ten years since I transplanted it from a wood near Dover; in the rainy January dusk, the rounded tufts of leaves have a dark metallic sheen, the whole plant is impressive and rather sinister, with its pale "mermaids' hands" clasping the drooping buds which, half-expanded, seem like the heads of adders poised to strike.

There is another English Hellebore, *Helleborus viridis*, which we shall encounter next month; but some of the foreign species of the genus are far more impressive than either of the British plants—notably the Christmas Rose, *Helleborus niger*, a native of southern Europe. Nor can I forbear to mention the magnificent Corsican Hellebore, *Helleborus corsicus*, like a vastly magnified Setterwort, with prickly edges to its leaves, which seems to have no very strong objection to the English climate, for it is naturalized in some gardens, and there is a fine plant, for instance, in the Fellows' Garden at Exeter College, Oxford.

January, I think, has a claim to be the most beautiful of the months—

a rash statement, for I am quite capable of saying the same of any of the others, given a propitious mood and a fine day. But January has an austere, almost a sculptural quality which suggests classical art: it stands by itself, aloof, the "still centre of the turning world"; untouched by either the deathly melancholy of December or the feverish unrest of February. To-day, under a high, clear sky, the fields and woods seemed as fixed and unchanging as some country scene in a Book of Hours: smooth, stylized, but seeming, in an odd way, more real than the reality. . . . Only at one other season, I think—the extreme end of August—does one experience this same sense of timelessness, the feeling of having come to a full-stop. But in August this timeless moment is heavy with the sense of fulfilment, of fruition; very different is the naked, athletic equilibrium of January, poised dangerously at the gateway of the year, heralding the spring's unrest and the long-drawn passion of the summer.

February

THE static, sculptural beauty of January dissolves in the lengthening evenings; "the days draw out"—hackneyed as the phrase is, it retains an indestructible poetry: muttered by the homing labourer, in the bright, clear evenings, it can still catch at the heart like an incantation, bringing spring suddenly nearer. Towards the end of January one does, in fact, begin to notice the longer twilight and the swelling buds: with the first of February, one is aware of the gap since Christmas— Time, which in the Janus-month seemed static, suspended, is moving on again.

> Over the land freckled with snow half-thawed
> The speculating rooks at their nests cawed
> And saw from elm-tops, delicate as flower of grass,
> What we below could not see, Winter pass.

Edward Thomas is extraordinarily sensitive to seasonal changes— it is noteworthy, too, how many of his poems are called by the names of the months. Poets, I suppose, are more weather-conscious nowadays than formerly—before the nineteenth century, weather in poetry was apt to be a rather conventional affair: poets preferred it to be fine— it would be hard, I imagine, to find many pre-Victorian poems in praise of rain—and May and June seem to have been top favourites.

February, I think, can dispute April's claim to be "the cruellest month,"

> mixing
> Memory and desire, stirring
> Dull roots with spring rain . . .

It is the febrile month, one is aware of the germ of spring invading the land slowly, like the onset of some insidious fever. . . . Suddenly, after a week of thaw and sleet, the wind blows soft, and one gets one of those miraculous days which seem to have been stolen from April or May: warm and languorous, with sculptured clouds riding the high, pale sky. The catkins shine out with a new radiance, one is startled, in the warm woodland silence, by a sudden buzz, as of a spent bullet, past one's ear—the first bee; or down some sheltered, sun-filled ride one will notice, incredulously, a flicker of sulphurous yellow among the dying fireworks of the catkins—the first brimstone butterfly.

The hazel catkins themselves are, as a matter of fact, precisely the colour of "flowers of sulphur," the purified form of the drug which, mixed with treacle, used to be popular in my childhood as a spring medicine (it was said to "clear the blood"). Flowers of Sulphur would, indeed, be a good name for the Hazel: the yellow "Lambs'-tails" have that faint greenish tinge which lurks in brimstone—quite distinct from the richer gold of Sallow Willow. . . . The sallow catkins now, in February, are still tight, silvery rabbit scuts: they will not reveal their glories till March. Picked and kept in water, they will grow lustily, however, and put out rootlets which, in a glass vase, look like those of epiphytal orchids. It is odd, by the way (catkins quite apart), that most spring flowers, at any rate in England, tend to be white or yellow: I can think of almost no red- or purple-flowered plant (except Red Deadnettle) which appears before April—and most of the brightly-coloured flowers wait till June. The reason is presumably a climatic one—one can't help feeling, at times, an unpatriotic nostalgia for the splendours of an Italian spring: the red and purple anemones, the crocuses and the rose-pink cyclamens.

There is, of course, one magnificent exception to the rule—the Mezereon, *Daphne mezereum*. Non-botanists are often surprised to learn that Mezereon (which gardeners will persist, with a maddening pedantry, in calling "Daphne") is a native British plant: many a time have I patriotically defended its claims against suburban incredulity. Recently, alas! I read somewhere that it is one of those plants which (like the Greater Celandine) are supposed to have been brought over by the Romans. . . . None the less, Mezereon can I think fairly be included, without cheating, in the British Flora. Only just—for nowadays it is excessively rare; I can't claim to have seen it growing wild myself, but I know botanists who have. To come upon its wax-pink, clustered sprays among the undergrowth of an English copse is one of several botanical treats which I have looked forward to all my life; but, like the Pasque Flower and *Orchis militaris*, the Mezereon has always eluded me, and will probably continue to do so. I almost hope that it does: once found, it would be one pleasure the less to look forward to; and if Mezereon is really the shrub into which Daphne so inconsiderately translated herself, one may be forgiven for distrusting so inconstant a nymph, who would probably be quite capable, if one ran her to earth, of changing her shape a second time—probably into a mere Spurge Laurel (another, duller *Daphne*), or Butcher's Broom.

In the eighteenth century she was less coy: Gilbert White seems to have taken quite for granted her presence at Selborne:

"*Daphne mezereum*, the mezereon" (he laconically records), "in Selborne Hanger among the shrubs at the south-east end above the cottages. . . ." On one occasion (he says) it was in bloom on the fifteenth of December; it will normally put out a flower or two in January; but February is its month. White's phrase "above the cottages" carries, for the botanist, a faintly sinister association: was Mezereon at Selborne an "escape from cultivation"? I prefer, myself, to think that the Mezereons so frequent, still, in cottage gardens, are escapes *into* cultivation: their progenitors have been, in all probability, uprooted from the neighbouring woodlands—and not only at Selborne; in my own district, East Kent, the plant is one of the commonest garden-shrubs. Mezereon *has* occurred, wild, in the neighbourhood—there are records, I think, in the *Flora of Kent*—but nowadays it is almost certainly extinct.

I have myself botanized on Selborne Hanger, but not at the right time of year for Mezereon. My only notable find was the Violet

Helleborine, long recorded from the locality. A friend and myself had bicycled over from Steep, on a pouring wet day in late July; we were drenched before we reached the top of the hanger. But there, sure enough, was the Violet Helleborine growing abundantly in the open, bushy spaces on the hill-top, just as the *Flora of Hampshire* had said it did. . . . At the very moment that we came upon it, the rain stopped, the hot July sun blazed down through the tree-tops, and (for it happened to be a Sunday) a Salvation Army band struck up a lively tune in the village below. . . . The occasion, we felt, could hardly have been better arranged.

Mezereon, I fancy, was never very common in English woods: most of the earlier floras put it down as "rare." Anne Pratt hazards a guess that it is "probably wild in Hampshire," adding that the name "Mezereon" is derived from the Persian *Madzaryoun*. Turner does not seem to have heard of it as a wild plant in England, nor does Gerarde— though the latter was familiar with it as a native of "most of the East countries," particularly Poland, "from whence" (he says), "I have had great plentie thereof for my garden." He adds that the leaves of Mezereon (or "Spurge Flaxe") "do purge downward, flegme, choler, and waterish humors with great violence. Also, if a drunkard do eate one graine or berrie of this plant, he cannot be allured to drinke any drinke at that time; such will be the heate of his mouth and choking in the throte."

Daphne laureola, the Spurge Laurel, also flowers in February: it is, so far as I know, an undisputed native of England, though rare in Scotland and apparently absent from Eire. It is fairly frequent in woods on chalk and limestone, and, with its evergreen leaves, is a not un- attractive little shrub, though the small, bell-shaped green flowers are a poor substitute for Mezereon. Oddly enough, however, this rather dim plant is supposed, in the "Language of Flowers," to signify "Coquetry, Desire to Please." Flowering "amid the snows of January" it seems, says one authority,[1] "the fitting representative of an impru-

[1] Robert Tyas: *The Language of Flowers* (1875).

dent coquette who, in the dead of winter, decks herself in Spring attire."

I have mentioned Butcher's Broom, that curious shrub which looks rather like a small holly-tree (one of its names is Knee Holly) and which is in fact (such are the vagaries of scientific classification) a lily. It is a pleasant sight in the winter woodlands, and frequent enough in the south, though (according to Bentham and Hooker) "not truly native" farther north. It is in several respects a paradoxical plant— not only is it (against all probability) a lily, but its curious, stiff, pointed "leaves" are not leaves at all, but cladodes—flattened, leaf-like stems, in the centre of which are borne the small, stellate green flowers and, afterwards, the large scarlet berries. The flowers appear in February, sometimes in January. According to Parkinson, the plant was used "to preserve hanged meate from Mise Eating, from whence came the *Italian* name of *Pongitopi*." It was also used, the same author tells us, "for to make Broomes to sweep the house, from whence came the name *Scopa regia*, but the King's Chamber is by revolution of time turned to the Butcher's stall, for that a bundle of the stalkes tied together, serveth them to clense their stalles, and from thence have we our English name of Butchers Broome."

If one is lucky one will come across, in February, the first violets— possibly the scented one, *Viola odorata*, though it is more likely to be the far commoner and, to my mind, quite as charming (though scentless) Dog Violet, *Viola canina*. Why, I wonder, was the prefix "Dog" used to imply inferiority? It is a surprising circumstance, surely, in a nation of dog-lovers. I suspect, however, that the totemistic dog-cult came in, like cold baths, the team-spirit and other "English" characteristics, with the nineteenth century. Shakespeare is singularly tepid in his admiration for dogs; Dr. Johnson definitely preferred cats, and most poets, I fancy, have shared his taste. I am surprised that nobody has yet written a monograph upon the psychological aspects of dog-worship in England. The parallels with Hinduism are obvious;

and one can only regret that the External Soul of the true blue Briton should have chosen to lodge itself in these yapping, snarling nuisances rather than in the placid, august and (relatively) harmless form of the Sacred Cow.

I was forgetting Cow Parsley—but it doesn't, I think, seriously affect the argument. . . . Another February flower which, like the Dog Violet, suffers from invidious comparisons, is the Barren Strawberry: not a strawberry at all, but a Potentilla, it is apt to lure one with false promises. The genuine wild strawberry, however, flowers later. Innocent of such deceitful wiles, and likely to be overlooked by all but the botanist, is the Spring Whitlow Grass, *Draba verna*: the smallest member of the Cabbage Family, it frequents dry banks and the tops of walls, which it covers with a sprinkling of white like a thin snowfall. Only two or three inches high, it is a charming little plant, and, if looked at through a large magnifying-glass, not inferior to Lady's Smock or some of its other more sizeable relations. According to Anne Pratt, it was formerly regarded with some suspicion by farmers who, she says, "used to imagine that when it appeared in any quantity, it foreboded short crops of corn in autumn." Miss Pratt herself, one feels, is properly sceptical about such legends; and in fact she hastens to assure us, by way of vindicating the plant's reputation, that "it flourishes at Tunbridge Wells"—surely a sufficient guarantee of respectability.

In the woods, towards mid-February, one notices the reddish, immature tassels of Woodspurge: its "cup of three" will not, however, be visible till April. The contrasted colouring of its foliage and its flower-clusters recalls the Setterwort, and the Woodspurge has many a time led me on a wild-goose chase. The other English "Christmas Rose," *Helleborus viridis*, makes its appearance in February or early March: unlike Setterwort, it is deciduous, and therefore less easy to spot out of season. The flowers are larger and wider open than *Helleborus fœtidus*, and nearer in shape to the Christmas Rose itself; they are of a pale, whitish green, without the Setterwort's thunderous purple fringe to the sepals. It is less rare than its more imposing relation,

34

but it is a local plant, and has to be searched for in likely places—in woods, mostly on the chalk. Culpepper mentions Northamptonshire as a favoured county. The Hellebores, he says, are Herbs of Saturn: "and therefore no Marvel if it hath some sullen conditions with it, and would be far safer, being purified by the Art of the Alchymist, than given raw. If any have taken any harm by taking it, the common Cure is to take Goat's Milk; if you cannot get Goat's Milk, you must make a shift with such as you can get." Not really very helpful—but Culpepper, one feels, would never have inspired much confidence as a family doctor; he lacked the proper bedside manner. The English Hellebore, he adds, as a consoling afterthought, "works not so churlishly as those do which are brought from beyond Sea, as being maintained by a more temperate Air." The roots, says Gerarde, "take away the morphew and black spots on the skin, tetters, ringwoormes, leprosies and scabs"—nor is this all, for a dram of the root, powdered, and boiled with Rue and Agrimony, "cureth the jaundise, and purgeth yellow superfluities by siege."

Moschatel, which I mentioned in January, should be in blossom by now; and one may (rather optimistically) begin to look for the first celandines and primroses. Coltsfoot, too, may make a welcome appearance this month, though it belongs really to March. An all-the-year-round plant which (though never really out of flower) takes on a new lease of life in February, is Shepherd's Purse—*Capsella bursa-pastoris*. More than Moschatel it deserves the name Adoxa—"without glory"; it is a troublesome weed in gardens but its small, cruciferous flowers, like those of the Whitlow Grass, can be pleasing when seen in the mass, on some dry sunny bank, in midwinter. Matthew Robinson, the early nineteenth-century herbalist, observes that the plant "is also called Shepherd's Scrip, Shepherd's Pouch, Toywort, Pickpurse, and Casewort." He adds that "it is astringent and glutinous," and good for "bleeding at the nose and spitting of blood, and in diarrhoes, dysentries and bloody urine." Made into a poultice and "applied to the wrists," it was also a cure for "ague": Robinson adds that it was to be applied "before the fit comes on," though he fails to explain how the

35

necessary prognosis was to be accomplished. The same treatment is recommended for erysipelas—and here again one infers that, to be effective, it must be begun before the onset of the disease.

Robinson's book, *The New Family Herbal*, is a curious work—a degenerate descendant of Gerarde and Culpepper surviving into the Victorian age. In his preface, the author acknowledges his debt to Culpepper "and those before his time," adding, however, that "a great portion of their works is entirely useless." He disposes at once of the astrological aspect of herbal medicine: "*The government of Herbs by the sun, moon, and planets*" (he declares) "has been exploded by modern science. . . . He who would now connect Astrology with Botany would stultify himself, and hold himself up to public contempt. . . . It would be the greatest folly to perpetuate the ignorance and absurdities of ancient Herbalists. . . ." Yet Dr. Robinson (for thus he styled himself), despite his claims to be up-to-date and scientific, proceeds to "perpetuate" most of the "absurdities" which he so pompously condemns. Astrology is barred; but his prescriptions are largely mediæval, he is more credulous than Culpepper, and, though rejecting the "government" of plants by the stars, appears to retain all the faith of his predecessors in the doctrine of "signatures": thus, he will recommend the root of Devil's-bit Scabious for the treatment of bites—a piece of pure sympathetic magic, having its origin in the fact that the scabious root appears, itself, to have been bitten.

How many such "cures," one wonders, are resorted to to-day? More, possibly, than one would think—and not only in those countries which are generally spoken of as "backward." . . . I myself have known herbalists in England, in recent years, whose credulity was almost equal to that of Dr. Robinson; the only difference seems to be that the tradition has become an oral (and largely "underground") one; herbalists, nowadays, do not usually commit their knowledge to print.

Incidentally, the account of Shepherd's Purse which I have quoted above is one of innumerable examples to be found in the herbals of plants from which, quite apart from the genuineness (or otherwise) of their "virtues," it must have been extraordinarily difficult to extract the essential juices. Shepherd's Purse is a particularly recalcitrant herb, one would have supposed; its thin, wiry stems and small leaves seem to contain almost no moisture whatever, and the mind boggles at the prospect of collecting enough of it (common though it is) to cure an attack of dysentery, or to make a poultice against the "ague."

The languorous, febrile days were a deception—a mere "vision of spring in winter"; rain blows up in the evening on the south-west wind, the lengthening twilight is full of the sound and smell of the rain, the birds sing in sudden shrill bursts through the windy down-pour. Next day, the wind is in the north-east, the rain turns to sleet, and the walls and banks which were powdered with Whitlow Grass or Shepherd's Purse are now flecked and dappled with a denser white-ness. February, as often as not, goes out like a lion—but in the high woods there is a "roaring peace," the sunset has a sudden, lucent clarity which has a hint of wildness, a suggestion that the equinox is not very far off. . . . In the cart-tracks, between the high hedgerows, the puddles catch the last brightness: "The days are drawing out," says the cow-man, plodding home through the muddy lanes. The catkins hang drenched, their sulphurous lustre gone; but in the morning, suddenly, a spark of brighter gold gleams from the chalk banks of the railway cutting: a fringed yellow star—the first Coltsfoot, an interloper, a flower of March.

March

> The boys are up the woods with day
> To fetch the daffodils away,
> And home at noonday from the hills
> They bring no dearth of daffodils . . .[1]

IN Shropshire, perhaps—but hardly in Kent. In the eastern counties there is a distinct and regrettable dearth of daffodils: I only know one locality for them in Kent, and here they are "fetched away" in thousands almost before they have a chance to bloom. The Daffodil is a true native, and may at one time have been commoner than it is to-day. The "Common yellow Daffodilly," says Gerarde (writing at the end of the sixteenth century), "groweth almost every where through England," but to-day it is a local plant, least infrequent, probably, in the West Country, where it can be depended upon to "take the winds of March with beauty"—though in Kent, after a hard winter, it may delay till April.

The Daffodil, like the Mezereon, is apt to escape *into* as often as *from* cultivation: personally I prefer the original "Lent Lily" to any of the larger, cultivated kinds, and only wish it were a more frequent invader. In spite of its romantic associations, *Narcissus pseudo-narcissus* is poisonous: "the blossoms," says Anne Pratt, in her little book on poisonous plants, "act as an emetic and have caused illness in children who ate portions of them." I was never tempted, in my childhood, to eat daffodils; but Victorian flower-books are full of such awful warnings, and daffodil leaves, adds Miss Pratt, "when boiled by mistake for leeks in soup, have caused suffering"—a mishap which, one is

---

[1] A. E. Housman: *A Shropshire Lad.*

tempted to surmise, may have occurred in Wales, where these two plants are ever apt to be confused.

The Daffodil is the true flower of March—the month when the sun "rides on the gold wool of the Ram." Yellow is March's colour: Daffodil, Coltsfoot, Celandine and "mealed-with-yellow sallows." . . . The sallow catkins, by the way, are in their glory by the end of the month: one comes upon them suddenly, at the wood's edge, an apocalyptic blaze of gold against the still-brown thickets. Hopkins' image has always, for me, something of the breath-taking vividness of the willow catkins themselves: indeed, whenever I think of this sonnet, I remember those "mealed-with-yellow sallows" to the exclusion of the rest, and am too liable to forget that the poem is, after all, called *The Starlight Night*, and that the sallows are a mere simile—like the

> Wind-beat whitebeam! airy abeles
> set on a flare!
> Flake-doves sent floating forth at
> a farmyard scare! . . .

This poem, indeed, like a good many of Hopkins', is overcrowded with visual images which, flashing forth one after another, with an electric intensity, tend to invalidate the total effect. Sallows, white-beams, "flake-doves"—one is overwhelmed by a positive sun-burst of imagery, and forgets all about the night and the stars after the first few lines.

March is the soldier's month—harsh, boisterous, masculine, yet capable of an almost feminine tenderness. The wind drops in the evening, and one is aware of a sudden softness in the air, a sense of promise: the birds sing with a new lustiness, the swollen chestnut-buds are taut to bursting, the rain-wet earth exhales the very smell of spring. The February days which, languorous and "out-of-season", called forth the brimstone butterfly and the first celandines, recur now with an intenser, more disquieting warmth: the celandines spread their stars along the hedge-bank and through the damp copses, among the flowering Dog's Mercury. Buttercups of a kind, they are more deserving of the name, I think, than the true Buttercups, *Ranunculus bulbosus* and *Ranunculus acris*. The Celandine's other name, Pilewort, seems in any case a pity: like the Orchises, it suffers from having a root which is apt to "put ideas into people's heads," though blameless enough above ground. The doctrine of signatures is, as usual, to blame: the clusters of tubers suggested, to the early herbalist, the form of hæmorrhoids, and the Celandine has long been famous as a cure for that distressing complaint. Curtis, writing towards the end of the eighteenth century (in his *Flora Londiniensis*), is already sceptical: "like many other remedies more rationally recommended" (he says), "it may palliate, but will scarcely effect a cure." None the less, Robinson, a generation later, continues to recommend the Celandine as "a wonderful remedy" not only for piles, but for "the king's evil, or any other hard wens or tumours."

According to Gerarde the cure seems to have been a fairly recent discovery in his day: "The later age" (he writes), "use the rootes and graines for the piles, which being often bathed with the juice mixed with wine, or with the sick mans urine, are drawne togither and dried up, and the paine quite taken away. There be also who thinke, that if the herbe be but caried about one that hath the piles, the paine forthwith ceaseth." With more confidence, he recommends that the juice "mixed with honey" be "drawne up into the nosthrils," as a means of purging the head of "foule and filthie humours."

As a cure for piles, the Celandine is, I suppose, by now entirely discredited; Anne Pratt, writing in the eighteen-sixties, says nothing of its former reputation as a medicine—an omission due, no doubt, to the prudishness of the times rather than to any ignorance on the part of Miss Pratt. "Children in country-places in Kent," she says, "rub their teeth with [the leaves], to improve their whiteness." She adds that these leaves "were formerly boiled and eaten; but the author, who has tried their worth, cannot say much in their favour." (I have not, myself, tried cooking celandine leaves, but I can strongly recommend them as a pleasant addition to a winter salad.)

Flower names are often ambiguous, and can cause lamentable confusion: nothing could be more unfortunate, for example, than the muddle over the two "celandines." The other "celandine," so called, *Chelidonium majus*, is a member of the poppy family—a squalid and unpleasant weed with a small orange flower; yet it is this plant which, as Mr. Andrew Young reminds us,[1] is carved on the Wordsworth Memorial at Grasmere—surely the very last flower to have evoked a poem, even if it were not perfectly evident, from the context, that Wordsworth meant *Ranunculus ficaria*; yet the name *Chelidonium* does suggest that the Greater Celandine may, after all, have a prior claim to the title.

Yellow is March's colour, as I have said, and nowhere is it more in evidence than on certain sea-cliffs, notably at Dover, which are brightened, towards the end of this month, by masses of Sea Cabbage and wild Wallflower.[2]

The Cabbage, *Brassica oleracea*, is a handsome plant, with its tall racemes of sulphur-yellow flowers, and its tough, glaucous leaves. These leaves hardly suggest that the wild plant is, in fact, the ancestor of all our garden cabbages, kales, coleworts and the rest. Anne Pratt who, like her contemporary Frank Buckland, seems to have been willing to try anything once, alleges that "repeated washings will fit this cabbage for use, and when boiled, it is a good vegetable." The boys of Dover, she adds, "occasionally gather it from the cliff, and carry it into the town for sale; but it does not seem to be much used in the neighbourhood, either by rich or poor." Dovorians, as I happen to know, are a pretty tough lot; but not even they, it seems, could stomach *Brassica oleracea*.[3] Even in Gerarde's day, it was not (as he says)

[1] *A Prospect of Flowers.*

[2] I shall perhaps be accused of "cheating" over the Cabbage, which may not be out till April; the Wallflower, however, is well in flower by mid-March.

[3] I have since been told that, in the absence of other "greens," the cabbage is still sold in Dover and Folkestone, at the exorbitant price of 8d. per pound.

"sought after as a meate; but is sowen and husbanded upon ditch bankes and such like places for the seede sake, by which often times great gaine is gotten." The "Sea Colewoort," he adds, "groweth naturally upon the bayche and brimmes of the sea . . . betweene Whyttable and the Ile of Thanet"—where doubtless it can still be found to-day.

The Wallflower, or "Yellow Stocke Gilloflower," as Gerarde calls it, is common enough on some sea-cliffs, and has also a penchant for ruins. Suspicions are often cast on its claims to be a true "native," but the wild Wallflower is easily distinguished from any "garden-escape": it is much smaller than any of the cultivated forms, and its colour is always uniformly yellow. Gerarde quotes Galen in praise of the plant's "clensing facultie," and Dioscorides, it seems, recommended it as a cure for "the choppes or riftes of the fundament."

As a Man of Kent, I am naturally attracted to those plants which seem (like the Lady Orchid and the Clove-scented Broomrape) to have a special predilection for my own county—and particularly for the eastern end of it. I cannot claim the Wallflower as an exclusively Kentish plant, nor even the "Sea Colewort," but these are not the only uncommon denizens of the Dover cliffs which, in later months, will harbour such rarities as the "Nottingham" Catchfly and the Picris Broomrape, not to mention several rare orchids. The Daffodil, as I have said, is a rare wildflower in the county: yet I notice that Miss Plues, in her *Rambles in Search of Wildflowers*, published in the eighteen-sixties, describes it as "half covering fields and groves in Kent." Those "groves" are suspicious, and suggest plantations—nor can I believe that the Daffodil has become nearly extinct in this region within less than a century. Miss Plues also alleges that she found the Poet's (or Pheasant's-Eye) Narcissus "wild in Durham, near the margin of a pond, and one specimen near Ross." Alas! *Narcissus poeticus* really isn't, whatever Miss Plues may say, a British plant—though Sowerby mentions that it was "gathered by Mr. Jacob Rayer on a rabbit-warren at Shorne, between Gravesend and Rochester, in flower May 26, 1795." So I can at least console myself with the thought that, if the Narcissus

43

ever had any claim to be a native, it was as much a flower of Kent as of anywhere else.

"The unusually mild winter of 185– had induced many families to pass it at the sea-side, and the inhabitants of Clevedon, in Somerset-shire, numbered more than the regular residents. Mrs. Dring, a widow lady, and her only daughter were occupying a handsome suite of rooms in one of the houses on the west of the town, and their Christmas had passed cheerily, enlivened by the society of two cousins, Esther Claridge, the eldest daughter of Mrs. Dring's brother, and Edward Leigh, the son of her sister.

"Two seasons in London, followed by gay autumns at watering-places, had made sad havoc with the health of Fanny Dring, and her pale face and attenuated figure, as she stood in the large bay window gazing wistfully on the lovely landscape, attracted her Mother's anxious observation. . . ."

The above passage is taken, not as one might suppose from a Victorian novel, but from the opening chapter of Miss Plues' *Rambles in Search of Wildflowers*, which I referred to just now. The book is, in fact, a kind of botanical tract, compiled for the benefit of girls like Fanny, with pale faces and "attenuated" figures, who have so far failed, despite "two seasons in London," to find husbands. . . . Fanny herself is plainly a problem: "I do not love idleness," she says, "and I am weary for want of an object for exertion." Cousin Esther, a blue-stocking who, one feels, had probably read Harriet Martineau and perhaps even (in the privacy of her boudoir) George Eliot, suggests that they form a botanical club, under her presidency. Cousin Edward, aged seventeen ("a brilliant scholar in a large public school in one of the midland counties") enthusiastically supports the scheme; he has, in fact, already been bitten by the bug: "I scarcely knew a Dandelion from a Buttercup when I came here, and now I know the Michaelmas Daisy, and the Sea Orache, and the Knot-Grass, and ever so many other things. . . ." The club is duly formed, and, when

44

the family disperse to their various homes, its activities are continued by post. . . . Between them, they contrive (very conveniently for the author's purpose) to discover most of the species in the British Flora, and a thoroughly good time is had by all, with the possible exception of poor Edward who, when he attempts to botanize at his public school, is promptly branded as a cissy: "When first the other day-pupils found that he was addicting himself to collecting flowers, they named him 'Miss Flora.' " One is glad to learn, however, that "the boy was largely endowed with firmness and held steadily to his purpose," and that "he declined ever replying to this cognomen."

I myself have a soft spot for Edward, having suffered in much the same way; moreover, he lived, like myself, in Kent—it was he who found the wild Daffodil there; he is credited, moreover, with finding Coralwort (*Dentaria bulbifera*), also in Kent—which is more than I have ever done. Miss Plues, as it happens, trips him up in a later paragraph, pointing out that the Coralwort was in fact discovered just over the Sussex border, "in some plantations on the estate of Lilles Den." Edward, one feels, though a somewhat erratic botanist, was acquainted with all the best people in his neighbourhood—though he may, of course, have been trespassing on this occasion.

Miss Plues, though her approach may appear frivolous, has, like her contemporary Miss Pratt, a proper sense of the seriousness of scientific pursuits; the bulk of her book comprises, in fact, a "beginner's" flora: the plants are described systematically, under their Natural Orders, and though not overburdened with technicalities, the descriptive sections were probably successful in their object—which was, as we have seen, to rouse the interest of debilitated young ladies like Fanny Dring. The personal note is sustained throughout: Edward finds the Dogwood at Hawkhurst (he could hardly have missed it), and Fanny herself, after "diligently" searching for *Orobanche rubra* at the Lizard, is "rewarded by a sturdy specimen." By the end of the book, Fanny appears to have made a complete recovery; and if the

45

Rambles do not, in fact, end with wedding-bells, one cannot help feeling that Edward and Fanny were obviously made for each other.

Another seaside plant, conspicuous in March, is Alexanders—it will scarcely be in flower till April, but the tufts of glossy, succulent-looking leaves are abundant on cliff-sides and banks on the south coast, and make a brave show at a time when most of the associated plants are still brown and leafless. The rounded umbels of yellowish flowers are less impressive than the leaves, and the whole plant, in its maturity, has the overblown, rather squalid air of so many of the *Umbelliferæ*. Taking their cue from the Hemlock, most people suppose all umbel-bearing plants to be poisonous—a reputation which is surely unfair to a family which includes the carrot, parsnip, celery, parsley and a number of other more or less indispensable vegetables. (I say "more or less" advisedly, for I should find it easy, myself, to dispense with the carrot, for instance, which seems to me defiantly uneatable, except when very young. On the other hand, why do we never cultivate the Fennel in this country? It is a delicious vegetable, either cooked or eaten raw, like celery).

Alexanders itself is, in fact, edible: try the young shoots, raw—or the leaves may be treated like "spring greens." Parkinson recommends the "tops of the rootes with the greene leaves," which were "used in Lent especially." Anne Pratt, though she quotes Parkinson in this connection, seems not to have tried Alexanders herself, which is unlike her: especially since the plant is extremely common at Dover, where she lived. "If I should set downe," Parkinson continues, "all the sortes of herbes that are usually gathered for sallets, I should not onely speake of garden herbes, but of many herbes which grow wilde in the fields, or else be but weedes in a garden; for the usuall manner with manie, is to take the young buds and leaves of every-thing, almost, that groweth, as well in the garden as in the fields, and put them all together, that the taste of the one may amende the relishe of the other."

One can't help wishing that Parkinson's method still prevailed in this country, where most people's idea of a salad is a limp, soggy lettuce drenched in vinegar. At the same time, the practice must have had its dangers—and doubtless led to some of those horrific cases of poisoning which Miss Pratt herself is so fond of describing.

Alexanders, according to Culpepper, was "effectual against the biting of serpents"; it was also useful to "break wind and provoke urine," besides being good for the liver and spleen. "And now," Culpepper concludes, in his customary, rather snooty manner, "now you know what *Alexander Pottage* is good for, that you may no longer eat it out of Ignorance, but out of Knowledge."

Whatever one may think of "Alexander Pottage"—personally, I have not tried it—or of Culpepper himself as a dispenser of herbal remedies, the fact remains that modern medicine is founded, to a great extent, upon the researches of the herbalists; a number of plants recommended by Culpepper, for instance, still retain their place in the pharmacopœia. Foxglove and Deadly Nightshade are typical of such survivals: the virtues of both are duly celebrated in the herbals, yet not more fulsomely than a number of herbs which, in modern medical practice, have become totally discredited—Betony, for example, which according to Antonius Musa, physician to the Emperor Claudius, was a specific remedy for forty-seven disorders. The magical repute of Betony was perpetuated by the herbalists up till quite recent days: in fact, it is probably still used by such "wise women" as may survive in the remoter countryside. Yet Betony has, it seems, no real medicinal value whatever, whereas Foxglove and Belladonna furnish two indispensable drugs—digitalis and atropine.

A border-line case is the Coltsfoot, *Tussilago farfara*. Famous within living memory as a "cough-cure," it was esteemed at an earlier period for a number of other maladies as well: Culpepper recommends it, not merely for "Cough, Wheezing, Shortness of Breath," but also for "Agues, Inflammations, Swellings, St. Anthony's Fire, Burnings,

47

Cholerick Pushes,[1] Piles, Inflammations in the Privities." For none of these alarming complaints would Coltsfoot now be considered a reliable remedy; it is still, however, used in the manufacture of "herbal" tobacco, and I am told that it can be added to ordinary blends with tolerable results—a useful economy nowadays, though few smokers, I imagine, take the trouble to practise it.

Coltsfoot, for me, is pre-eminently the flower of March—more so than the daffodil which, as a child, I didn't encounter in the wild state. Often passed over as a "dandelion," Coltsfoot is a trimmer, tidier flower than the more coarse-growing *pissenlit*, and its habit of flowering before the leaves appear makes it more conspicuous. It has a pre-dilection for railway-cuttings, and will thrive on ash-tips and rubbish-heaps where even the Dandelion can scarcely find a roothold. Always to be found in the suburbs, it has spread, since the blitz, into central London. Curtis mentioned it (1799) as growing "in *Charlton Sandpits*, and many other places about Town"; it is, I suppose, one of the few records in the *Flora Londiniensis* which can still be confirmed by modern botanists.

The Coltsfoot, though often called a "dandelion," is in fact more like a daisy, having both disk-florets and ray-florets. Its curious "scape," clothed with brownish scales, is also a distinguishing feature, suggesting, before the flowers expand or the leaves appear, that the plant is saprophytic, like the Fir-rape and some of the orchids. Coltsfoot, indeed, is something of an oddity, though a charming one. It is perhaps surprising that it has been so little celebrated by poets—it is not less attractive, surely, than the Celandine. True, Bishop Mant has some lines about it—but then there must be few British wild plants which do not occur in his Collected Works:

> O'er scaly stem, with cottony down
> O'erlaid, its lemon-colour'd crown
> Which droop'd unclosed, but now erect
> The Coltsfoot bright develops . . . etc., etc.

[1] I am informed by a correspondent that "push" is good East Anglian for a boil or pustule.

A methodical anthologist (which I am not) could probably discover other poems about the Coltsfoot—possibly in Clare or Crabbe; and I cannot but think that Wordsworth mentioned it, though the reference, if any, eludes me.

I have remarked, already, how many flowers of early spring tend to be white or yellow; and the colours of March are still fairly subdued, though there are a few exceptions. I can think of three *blue* flowers in bloom this month: none of them very spectacular, yet all worth a glance. Of the Speedwells, the one which one is most likely to find in March is the ivy-leaved species—*Veronica hederifolia*: rather a dim little "Bird's-eye," and lacking the heavenly blue of the Germander Speedwell or of that other common species which has the horrible name of *Veronica Buxbaumii*. Druce, in *Hayward's Botanist's Pocket-book* (a useful and mainly accurate flower-guide) gives March-to-May as the flowering season of *Veronica hederifolia*, and firmly asserts that no other Speedwell flowers before April. I think that Druce, for once, is wrong—I have certainly found *Veronica Buxbaumii* in March, and I think *Veronica chamaedrys* as well, though they may have been "freaks."

Speedwell is one of those plants which, like Red Deadnettle, is apt to be passed over as a "weed" later in the year; but on a sunny day in March, in the hedgerow or on the borders of fields, its tiny blue flowers seem like fallen fragments of the cold, spring sky. . . . Less impressive, perhaps, though not less charming, is the Ground Ivy or Ale-hoof—my second blue flower of March. Its small flowers are easy to miss, but occasionally it occurs in such quantity that the whole woodland floor is tinged with its dull, purplish-blue. The leaves are faintly aromatic: according to one writer, "When rubbed on the under side, they have a pleasant smell; the upper side has none." There seems no reason to doubt the truth of this; yet it must surely be difficult to rub a Ground Ivy leaf on one side and not on the other. I cannot say that I have tried; my only source for this curious piece of information is a little book published anonymously in 1828, *Conversations on Botany*. The author (or rather, as one guesses from internal evidence, the authoress) was most certainly a "Lady," and quite possibly "A Lady of Title"; her book is arranged in dialogue form, like "Mrs Markham," and is extremely informative, if a trifle austere. ("What is Botany?" asks little Edward, rather pertly, and Mamma graciously proceeds to answer the question through the ensuing two hundred and forty pages.)

The odd name of "Ale-hoof" is not easily explained: nor, for that matter, are some of the plant's other names—Culpepper gives Turn-hoof, Haymaids and Gill-go-by-the-ground as alternatives. The surviving common name, Ground Ivy, seems itself to be rather lacking in point—the leaves are roughly ivy-shaped, but not more so than those of a good many other plants. Rather surprisingly, the Ale-hoof is a Herb of Venus, and is therefore recommended by the herbalists for the kind of complaints one might expect. It was also considered "good to tun up with new Drink, for it will clarify it in a Night."

My third blue flower is Periwinkle—*Vinca minor*, the lesser species; *Vinca major* is not a true native. Chaucer's "fresshe pervinke, rich of hewe" strikes me as an odd description of this flower: the clear, pale blue is not of a shade, I should have thought, to suggest richness. One wonders—as one wonders with so many of the older writers' references to flowers—whether Chaucer really meant the plant which we call Periwinkle. Yet all the evidence suggests that he did: "pervinke" is obviously the same as the French *pervenche*, which is still used in France for *Vinca minor* and *major*.

In the "language of flowers" Periwinkle stands for "Pleasing Remembrances"—it is hard to see exactly why, though Robert Tyas, whom I've quoted already, apparently derives the association from no less a person than Rousseau who, in his *Confessions*, relates how, when botanizing with Madame de Warens, that rather formidable lady exclaimed suddenly: "*Voilà de la pervenche encore en fleur.*" Not for thirty years did Rousseau encounter the Periwinkle again; then, "in 1764, being at Gressien, with my friend, M. du Peyron . . . I began

50

to botanize a little . . . and looking round among the bushes, I uttered a cry of joy, 'Oh! *voilà de la pervenche!*' And so indeed it was. . . ."

For myself, too, Periwinkle has a faint flavour of nostalgia—yet it is one of those curious *cafards* which seem to spring from no definite source; comparable, perhaps, with the emotion excited in the young Proust by the mysterious group of trees near Balbec. Yet I was never, I think, much attached to the Periwinkle in my childhood; *Vinca major* grew in our garden at Sandgate, but it was not one of those plants which made a special appeal to my imagination. Yet nowadays, whenever I come upon it, I am apt to cry excitedly, like Rousseau: "*Oh! voilà de la pervenche!*" and, like Proust before his three trees, I am aware of some elusive, unseizable image of happiness imprisoned among the dark, glossy leaves—even as the pale flowers themselves lurk, half-concealed, beneath their shade of green. The secret is, so to say, "on the tip of my tongue"—for a moment I seem to have grasped it; then it has vanished again, irretrievably, like a forgotten word, or the image of a dream. . . . All that remains is a vague impression of something delicate, innocent, virginal:

> The notion of some infinitely gentle
> Infinitely suffering thing.

The Greater Periwinkle is not, as I have said, a true native, though it often has every appearance of being perfectly at home in plantations and on hedgebanks. Curtis, in the *Flora Londiniensis*, records it from "a field near Beckenham, in Kent, where" (he says) "it was certainly in a wild state." The lesser species, according to the same writer, grew in "a field on the left side of Lordship Lane near Dulwich"; it is hardly likely to be found there nowadays, but *Vinca minor* is still a not uncommon plant "by the Hedge-Sides, in divers Places of this Land," as Culpepper remarks. It has the annoying habit, in many places, of producing an abundance of foliage but few (or no) flowers.

The medical and magical properties of Periwinkle seem not to have been very noteworthy: Hogg and Johnson, in their *Wild Flowers of Great Britain*, quote Bacon as saying that "it was common for people to wear bands of green periwinkle round the calves of their legs, to keep away the cramp." I have not verified this reference, but in his essay on Gardens, Bacon mentions "Periwinckle, the White, the Purple and the Blewe." White and purple forms are, I imagine, always cultivated—though Culpepper considered the white one to be wild. Periwinkle, according to him, was a herb of Venus, and "the Leaves eaten by Man and Wife together, Cause Love between them." It was also "a great Binder, [and] stayeth Bleeding both at Mouth and Nose, if some of the Leaves be chewed." Moreover, it was commended by Dioscorides, Galen and Aegineta "against the Lasks, and Fluxes of the Belly, to be drank in Wine."

Whether lion or lamb-like in its departure, March is the last winter month: spring, indeed, begins officially on the twenty-first, the vernal equinox—though the last days of the month are apt to be far from spring-like. This is the season of "Blackthorn Winter"; the scatter of sloe-blossom always astonishes one by the suddenness of its appearance, as though it were indeed sky- and not earth-born. It is said by some people to be unlucky to bring the Blackthorn indoors, but I think there is a confusion here with the Hawthorn, which is associated with the Great Plague: its odour is said to preserve the putrescent sweetness of what Harrison Ainsworth (in *Old St. Paul's*) pompously calls the "pestilential effluvium." But Blackthorn, so far as I know, has no such unpleasant associations.

Dog's Mercury and Moschatel now clothe the woods, and the green spears of bluebell-leaves are lengthening; the Cuckoo-pint, which pierced the beech-mast in January, with its burnished javelins, has now unfurled into clusters of large, glossy leaves which have an exotic, orchidaceous air. In an early season, primroses will be abundant enough to pick, but they are still short and stubby, and to gather a sizeable bunch is a laborious business.

The true flower of the spring equinox is the Wood Anemone or Windflower. One is tempted, indeed, to call it the first "spring" flower, according to official reckoning; its predecessors were winter flowers, though one can hardly deny the Coltsfoot's claim to be a flower of spring. No English wild flower makes a more dramatic first appearance than the Anemone; like the Blackthorn, its approach is sudden and unheralded: a few days since, the woodland floor was bare, now it is covered, whole acres of it, with the crowded, paper-thin flowers. The white carpet is like a sudden snow-fall, but the "snow" remains motionable and quivering, as though each flake hovered separately a few inches above the ground; and these suspended, tremulous flakes are stained, here and there, with a rosy blush, like the tinge of the sunset catching some alpine peak. Most exquisite of English flowers, the Anemone is one of the most fleeting: like Housman's Lent-lily, "it dies on Easter Day"—or very soon after. Its season is the equinox, the borderland season "bytuene Mershe and Averil," when "Spray biginneth to springe," and

> The lutel foul hath hire wyl
> On hyre lud to synge.

If March is the soldier's month, the male month, April is surely all feminine: and the Anemone is the flower of their union, androgynous, trembling between the two worlds of Winter and Spring.

April

APRIL is the "cruellest month" in more senses than one: the first warm days are too often delusive, north-east winds and sleet-storms ravage the plum-blossom and the wild cherry, Easter may be as "white" as a Dickensian Christmas. Even in childhood, I thought the spring a profoundly melancholy season, and the Church seemed rather to confirm my view, for my favourite Easter hymns tended to be extremely doleful: in particular, that one which begins:

> Jesus lives! No longer now
> Can thy terrors, death, appal us . . .
>   etc.

The tragic impression was increased, for me, by the fact that the first line, as it was sung, always sounded like:

> Jesus–lives–no–longer–now

—an interpretation which, though theologically inexact, seemed to me entirely suited to the seasonal mood. . . . As a child, I was chronically subject to these fits of romantic melancholy, from which I derived a peculiar and rather guilty pleasure: I learnt to indulge the sensation quite consciously, it became a kind of vice which I practised in the strictest privacy—not because I was particularly ashamed of it, but because I was quite certain that nobody would "understand."

April was, from earliest days, my favourite month: at the turn of the year, in January, I began to look forward to it; and April the First (quite apart from the fun of making April Fools of people) had always for me a holiday air, as though it were a kind of extra birthday. I had fixed ideas about the weather, and fully expected that the

first day of April would be showery: often it was not; but I remember that one year, after a week of dry, sunny weather, the day of days dawned punctually with drenching rain. The year was 1918: the fact has stuck in my memory, I suppose, because it was one of those very rare occasions when the English climate behaves according to one's preconceived ideas.

Primroses—and even bluebells—may flower in March, but the early Purple Orchid, for me the type-flower of April, will seldom be out much before the second or third week of the month—and perhaps not till later still. It is contemporary with—or slightly earlier than—the bluebells, among which its upright, gaudy spikes are conspicuous. They are always scattered, there were never (when one was a child) quite enough of them—this was so, at least, in the Kentish woods which I chiefly knew. Since then, I've seen the Early Purple growing in Cornish hedgerows in such abundance that one could have picked whole handfuls of it at a time. . . . As a matter of fact, *Orchis mascula* is apt to prove unpopular when brought indoors; its "catty" odour, often not noticeable in the open air, becomes all too evident in a warm room.

Linnæus, in naming the plant *Orchis mascula*, seems over-anxious to insist upon its maleness: the generic name, *Orchis*, is surely masculine enough by derivation, without the specific epithet. The twin tubers of the various *Orchises* (and other genera in the order) have acquired for these plants, from earliest antiquity, an entirely undeserved reputation as "herbs of Venus" (in the strictly practical sense of the term). Pliny mentions "satyrion" as an aphrodisiac, and Petronius describes it as being used in the lupanars. It is yet another—and very obvious—case of sympathetic magic; moreover, it has survived longer than most kindred superstitions, for orchis roots were sold in England, under the guise of "Salep," well into the nineteenth century—not, indeed, with any overt aphrodisiac intention, but merely as a "nourishing" food. No doubt the starchy, farinaceous element in the tubers had a certain amount of food value; but one can't help feeling that the plant's earlier repute had something to do with its later use as a substitute for sago.

"The roots of this [*Orchis mascula*] and the Green-winged Meadow Orchis" (writes Anne Pratt) "furnish the substance called 'Salep,' which was long imported from Turkey and other parts of the Levant, until it was discovered that our native plants could supply it. Salep is little used now in this country; but, less than a century since, the Saloop-house was much frequented, and the substance was a favourite repast of porters, coal-heavers, and other hard-working men. . . . It is still much used in Eastern countries; and a friend of the author's, long resident in India, remarks in a letter: 'Many a good basin of the thick salab gruel, prepared from the ground dried root of an Indian Orchis, have I swallowed, and found highly nutritious.' "

Salep is still sold in Turkey, I believe, and is there considered to be mildly aphrodisiac. Another species, not mentioned by Miss Pratt, which was used in its manufacture, is *Orchis militaris*, the Military Orchid, now nearly extinct in this country.

The primroses are at their best, in an average year, by the second week in April. As Culpepper remarks, "they are so well-known, that they need no description"; they are, in fact, the English "spring flower" *par excellence*, and possess, even for the most inveterate of townsmen, a symbolic significance which has nothing to do with Disraeli. One can't help wondering why the Primrose, rather than any other flower, acquired this aura of national sentiment. Not that I have the least desire to decry it: no English wild flower is more charming; but others seem to me quite as attractive—the Windflower, for instance, or the Bluebell; yet neither of these equally common flowers has, for the average person, the potently evocative quality of the Primrose. It is, for instance, almost the only wild flower which is ever sold in the London streets: the tight, pathetic little bunches are the first intimation, to most Londoners, that spring has really begun. One reason, perhaps, for the Primrose's popularity is that it a good traveller, and will survive for a considerable time without water; the same cannot be said for bluebells or anemones.

"The Cowslips and Primroses," says Gerarde, "are in temperature dry, and a little or nothing hot. The roots of the primrose," he adds, "stamped and strained, and the juice sniffed into the nose with a quill, or such like, purgeth the brains, and qualifieth the paine of the migrime." The yellow flowers and somewhat mealy leaves led botanists of Gerarde's day to include primroses and cowslips in the same family as the Mulleins—"for that the ancients have named them *Verbasculi*, that is to saie, small Mulleins." To the layman, this would seem, perhaps, at least as reasonable as many post-Linnæan classifications— who would suppose, for instance, at first glance, that the Larkspur and the Buttercup belonged to the same Natural Order?

The Primrose is no longer, I imagine, included in the British Pharmacopœia, and is indeed (perhaps fortunately) of no economic use whatever—even cows, it seems, won't crop it. "Pretty flower as it is," says Mrs. Lankester, in her *Wild Flowers Worth Notice*,[1] "all animals reject it as food excepting the pig. It seems, however, not wholly objected to by man, or woman either, for I lately saw a receipt for a primrose-pudding. A kind of wine, too, is made from the flowers, something like cowslip wine, but more delicate in flavour."

The scent of a freshly-gathered bunch of primroses is, in fact, faintly vinous—rather like the bouquet of a very old vintage port. Anne Pratt, in a lyrical essay on the Primrose, comments on the curious fact that Parkinson, Gerarde and other old writers refer to it as "green." Yet perhaps it is not so curious, after all: one thinks of the Primrose as yellow, certainly, but the impression is derived, chiefly, from the darker patches at the centre of the flower; the petals themselves are so pale as to be almost "off-white," and such colour as they possess shows a decidedly greenish tinge, rather resembling that of hazel catkins.

Cowslips, like wild daffodils, are commoner in the West Country

[1] London, 1861.

than in eastern England: in Kent they are rather scarce. The Oxlip is a rare plant, to be found only in a few localities in East Anglia; "Oxlips" found elsewhere are almost certain to be hybrids of cowslip and primrose. One suspects that the name Oxlip was once applied to some other plant, for Shakespeare and others refer to it as a common wild flower; possibly they meant the Cowslip, or perhaps they merely thought Oxlip a prettier name. The true Oxlip is common enough elsewhere in Europe, particularly in Switzerland; like the Primrose, however, it becomes rarer farther south, and I have not seen it in Italy, though the Primrose occurs as far south as the Abruzzi, where it is, however, rather rare. I remember finding, near Vasto, a single patch of it—a curiously nostalgic *trouvaille*, which seemed more exciting, at the time, than all the surrounding splendours of an Italian spring.

Talking of Italy, the Blue Mountain Anemone, *Anemone apennina*, which fills the Italian copses, is sometimes counted as a British plant, though it is a "doubtful native," and suspiciously fond of plantations. Curtis records it as growing "plentifully in Lord Spencer's Park at Wimbledon," and he adds that, though "we never could make it succeed in our garden at Lambeth-Marsh," it appeared to "thrive greatly" at Brompton.

The bluebells should be out by mid-April, but not yet in their prime: short and stubby still, they make a pleasant addition to a bunch of primroses, and, at this early stage, the blue has a deeper, more purplish tinge than when the flowers are fully expanded. Gerarde refers to the Bluebell as "Blew English Hare-Bels," and the "true" Harebell, *Campanula rotundifolia*, is still, as everyone knows, the Bluebell of Scotland. The roots of bluebells, says Gerarde, "boiled in wine and drunke . . . helpeth against the venemous bitings of the fielde spider," and according to Dioscorides they were also useful to "procure haire in beardlesse men, and such as have been overtaken with *Alopecia*." The botanical names *Hyacinthus non-scriptus, Agraphis nutans* and *Scilla non-scripta*, which have been applied to the plant by various authorities, refer one and all to the absence, in this species, of the leaf-markings attributed to the classical Hyacinth, which were supposed to commemorate the tragic death of Hyacinthus. Since nobody, however, has ever succeeded in identifying the original Greek plant, the distinction seems rather supererogatory. The Fritillary and (even) the Turk's-cap Lily have been suggested as alternatives: the bestowal of the name Hyacinth upon the Bluebell appears to have been arbitrary in the extreme.

In the hedges, the flowers which made a shy, unobtrusive appearance in February or March, are now in full bloom: Red and White Dead-nettle, Ground Ivy and the various Chickweeds. Among the latter, one can (if rather unkindly) count the Stitchwort, *Stellaria holostea:* it is not strictly a chickweed, but the two genera *Stellaria* and *Cerastium* are very closely related. Its white, fragile stars are scattered abundantly along the hedge, gleaming with a spectral whiteness among the darker foliage. Stitchwort is the most fragile, invalid-ish of plants: it cannot even stand up, but has to lean against its stronger neighbours. The narrow, grass-like leaves are of a pallid, rather "æsthetic" shade of green, and the flower itself of a pinched, wizened whiteness. One old name for it, apparently, was "All-bonie"—"whereof," says Gerarde, "I see no reason, except it be by the figure *Antonomia*, as when we say in English, He is an honest man, our meaning is, that he is a knave. For undoubtedly, this is a tender herbe. . . . Wherefore I take it to be so called by contraries." The seed, "being drunke," adds Gerarde, quoting Dioscorides, "causeth a woman to bring forth a man child, if after the purgation of her sicknes before she conceive, she do drinke it fasting thrise in a day . . . many daies together." It seems an arduous method of producing cannon-fodder: perhaps, like the name "All-bonie" it operated "by the figure *Antonomia*," in other words by a kind of anti-sympathetic magic.

Beaked Parsley, whose leaves have been visible since December, now forms dense thickets in hedge and orchard: it will hardly be in bloom, however, before the end of the month. Another common hedgeside plant for which I have a certain fondness is Jack-by-the-Hedge, also called Sauce Alone and Garlic Mustard. The "Garlic" refers to the smell of the leaves—a curious anomaly, for Jack-by-the-Hedge is far removed from the true Garlics, and in fact belongs to the cabbage family. Its dark green, rounded leaves are rather handsome, and the tall clusters of small white flowers are pretty in an unobtrusive way. According to Robinson (*Family Herbal*) the plant was eaten "by many country people as sauce to their salt fish, and wonderfully warms the stomach and promotes digestion."

> But e'en now the earth was cold,
>   Brown and bare as it could be;
> Not an orchis to be seen,
> Not a hooded arum green,
>   Not a ficary . . .

I quote this stanza from Mary Howitt (the poem was printed in *The Juvenile Forget-me-not* for 1836) for the sake of that "ficary" in the last line. It defeated me on a first reading; then I realized that it must refer to the Celandine, *Ranunculus ficaria*. So far as I know, "ficary" is entirely Miss Howitt's invention: she needed a rhyme, and the word just came to her. It seems a pity that it has not passed into general use.

Ficaries, by mid-April, are in their prime, or getting slightly over. The "hooded arum green," however, will be abundantly in flower by the end of the month: its names are legion—Cuckoo-pint, Wake-robin, Lords-and-Ladies, Jack-in-the-pulpit, Priest's Pintle, Calf's-foot, Ramp, Friar's Cowl, Starchwort, etc., etc. The last on the list—Starchwort—refers to the starchy substance formerly extracted from the root. This was held in considerable esteem in the days of starched ruffs, but, says Gerarde, it was "most hurtfull for the hands of the laundresse that hath the handling of it, for it choppeth, blistereth, and maketh the hands rough and rugged, and withall smarting." A substance called "Portland Sago" (to which I have already referred) was also made from Cuckoo-pint roots; its production no doubt proved uneconomic, for the roots had to undergo a somewhat lengthy and complex process before they were fit for human consumption—and even then, one imagines, they cannot have been very appetizing. Cuckoo-pint, indeed, seems to have been more suited to the stomachs of wild beasts than to those of human beings: "Beares," says Gerarde, "after they have lien in their dens forty daies without any maner of sustenance (but what they get with licking and sucking their owne feete) do as soone as they come foorth, eate the herbe Cuckowpint; through the windie nature whereof the hungrie gut is opened and made fit againe to receive sustenaunce. . . ."

In the woods, a number of less familiar plants are appearing among the primroses and the first bluebells: Ramsons, the common Wild Garlic, is often abundant, though somewhat local in its distribution. Its clusters of starry white blossom are delicious, its odour distinctly less so; the leaves are almost exactly like those of the Lily-of-the-Valley, and if one happens to be hunting for the latter (a rare plant in the wild state) Ramsons too often raises false hopes—but only for so long as one avoids treading on it. Even for those who like Garlic, the flavour of Ramsons is said to be too strong for culinary purposes, though Gerarde remarks that the leaves "may very well be eaten in April and Maie with butter, of such as are of a strong constitution and laboring men." One has often heard that the Elizabethans were tough; to anybody who has ever sniffed a leaf of Ramsons, Gerarde's words should remove all doubts in the matter. According to Anne Pratt, the plant was sometimes called Ramsies, Bear's Garlic and Buckrams.

Wood Sorrel is another woodland plant less well-known than it should be: it is shy, and apt to hide itself, but the delicate, drooping pink flowers are charming, though it is useless to try taking them home, for they wither almost at once. The leaves are pleasantly acid, and can be added to salads, though if eaten in vast quantities would presumably prove fatal, since oxalic acid is extracted from them. A plant of Venus, Wood Sorrel was effective, says Culpepper, "to procure an appetite," and "very excellent in any contagious sickness or pestilential fever." It is also one of the innumerable plants supposed to have been used by St. Patrick to demonstrate the nature of the Trinity. In fact, the true "Shamrock" has yet to be identified, and was far more probably some kind of clover, unless St. Patrick happened to be preaching in the middle of a wood. . . . "Among the Druids," says Mrs. Lankester, "its triple leaflets were regarded as a mysterious symbol of a trinity, the full meaning of which was involved in darkness." Mrs. Lankester herself does nothing to lighten the gloom by quoting a Welsh proverb of hermetic obscurity:

> Three things let no one trust such as shall dislike them,—
> The scent of trefoils, the taste of milk, the song of birds.

> Loveliest of trees, the cherry now
> Is hung with bloom along the bough—

and not only the Cherry, but the Chestnut, too, will be out by the end of the month, as well as the Wayfaring Tree, though this is only common in chalky districts. The wild Plum, I think, can dispute Housman's claim for the Cherry as the "loveliest of trees"; so too, perhaps, can the Hawthorn. Other possible candidates are the Crab Apple and the Guelder Rose.

Red Campion may be out by now, but is really, I think, a May flower, though it has a long flowering season, and lingers on into the autumn. Associated with it, though very different, is the Yellow Archangel, sometimes called Weasel-snout. It is, in fact, a Deadnettle, taller and handsomer than the red or white species, and common in most woods—in Curtis's day, it was "tolerably plentiful in *Charlton*," and can still be found within twenty miles of London.

I spoke of the Purple Orchids in Cornwall, and two Cornish plants, both rarities, are worth mentioning—Vernal Squill, and *Allium triquetrum*, another species of Garlic. The Squill is a pretty little bluebell with corymbs of purplish blue flowers, abundant on the Cornish cliffs, and extending up the west coast as far as the Orkneys. The Garlic, with racemes of starry white flowers, is abundant in Cornish hedge-rows: my first sight of it was from a car and, not knowing what it was, I jumped out and gathered a handful. A few minutes later the car was filled with an odour which could only be compared with the breath of an Italian peasant after a particularly hearty *festa. Allium triquetrum*, alas! had to be dropped out of the window.

Another April rarity, though not a Cornish one, is the wild Tulip: I must confess to never having found it, myself, in England, though I've seen it growing abundantly in Italian cornfields. It is truly wild, I believe, in East Anglia, and more doubtfully in one or two other districts. It's not very much like a tulip—the yellow flower is rather small, and inclined to droop, and the leaves are narrower than the garden species. It is one of the great prizes for an English botanist: I have not only not found it myself, but have met nobody who even claimed to have done so. Yet it continues to be recorded at rare intervals (like some of the nearly extinct orchids), so there's still a chance that I may come upon it some day.

On the chalk-downs, April flowers are rather scarce: the little spring sedge, *Carex caryophyllea*, is abundant, and with its brown glumes and bright yellow pollen has led me many a dance, for at a distance it looks like a Spider Orchid. The orchid itself, though a rarity, is fairly abundant on a few chalk-hills and cliffs in south-eastern England: it is more like a bee than a spider, and is often confused with the far commoner Bee Orchid. The sepals of the Spider, however, are green, whereas those of the Bee are bright purplish-pink. In the "language of flowers" the Spider Orchid signifies "skill," a singularly recondite piece of symbolism, referring to Arachne's dexterity at the loom.

Milkwort may be in flower on the downs: one of those pleasant flowers (and there are not many—Comfrey is another) which seem never to have made up their minds what colour they want to be. Milkwort is usually blue, sometimes pink and occasionally white: there are several species, all very similar, some of them rare. "Milke woort," says Gerarde, "is called *Ambarvalis flos*: so called bicause it doth specially flourish in the Crosse or Gang weeke, or Rogation weeke; of which flowers, the maidens which use in the countries to walke the procession, do make themselves garlands, and nosegaies: in English we may cal it Crosse flower, Gang flower, Rogation flower, and Milke Woort, of their virtues in procuring milke in the brests of nurses."

The connection between Milkwort and the Rogation-tide processions is obscure; a number of writers besides Gerarde refer to it. Anne Pratt, as so often, makes it an occasion for a little homily about the decline of piety: "Like so many other customs of those days," she remarks, "innocent and even laudable in themselves, they soon became perverted to seasons of revelry. That such was the case with Rogation ceremonies, both the old poems and sermons of those days abundantly prove. In one of the latter, the preacher exclaims, 'Alacke for pitie, these solemn and accustomable processions be nowe growen into a right foule and detestable abuse; so that the most part of men and women do come forth rather to set out and shew themselves, and to passe the time with vague and unprofitable tales and merrie fables, than to make generall supplications and prayers to God for their lacks and necessities.'"

The general conclusion seems to be that the "Gang Flower" was used on these "solemn and accustomable" occasions merely because it happened to be in bloom: but why pick on the small, insignificant Milkwort among so many other more showy and decorative plants in flower at that season? Plainly there were other reasons: Gerarde's remark about the plant's "virtues in procuring milke" suggests that Milkwort may have been regarded, at an earlier date, as a symbol of fertility. In any case, nothing will make me believe that village wenches in the sixteenth century were in the habit of gathering it purely for æsthetic reasons.

Another spring flower of the chalk-downs, far more worthy (one would have thought) to be carried in processions, is the Pasque Flower, *Anemone pulsatilla*. This lovely anemone, with its big blossoms of dark, smoky purple, is abundant on a few hills in southern England, but it is exceedingly local. I have never found it myself: I know where it grows, but I've never managed to be in the right place at the right time. "Pasque Flower" was Gerarde's name for the plant: "They flower for the most part about Easter, which hath mooved me to name it *Pasque Flower*, or Easter Flower." In his day, it grew "very plentifully in the pasture or close belonging to the personage house of a small village sixe miles from Cambridge, called Hildersham; the parson's name that lived at the impression heereof was Master *Fuller*, a very kinde and loving man, and willing to shewe unto any man the saide close, who desired the same."

In its fruiting stage, Pasque Flower is hardly less attractive than when in flower: "there succeedeth," says Gerarde, "an head or knoppe, compact of many graie hairie lockes, and in the solide parts of the knops lieth the seede flat and hoarie, every seede having his own small haire hanging at it." The Pasque Flower, like the Primrose, is beautiful but quite useless: "they serve onely for the adorning of gardens and garlands." In fact, the plant is poisonous, and cattle have been injured "and even killed," says Miss Pratt, "by cropping the Pasque Flower." I have been told that *Anemone pulsatilla* is in some districts called Daneflower, and was believed to have sprung from the blood of Danish invaders. This legend is more commonly associated (for no obvious reason) with the Dwarf Elder, *Sambucus ebulus*; the Pasque Flower is surely the more deserving candidate—a parallel case is the crimson Anemone of southern Europe and Asia Minor, supposed to have sprung from the blood of the wounded Adonis.

I must mention one more April rarity—*Fritillaria meleagris*, the Fritillary or Snake's-head Lily, a haunter of water-meadows in Oxfordshire and a few other counties. I don't know why it should have remained so local, since it is usually abundant where it occurs. Presumably its popularity as a cultivated flower has something to do with it: it seems to have been coveted by gardeners at an early date. "The chiefe or onely use thereof," says Parkinson, "is to be an ornament for the gardens of the curious lovers of these delights, and to be worne of them abroad, which for the gallant beauty of many of them, deserveth their courteous entertainment, among many other the like pleasures."

The dusky, chequered bells, trembling on their slender flower-stalks, have a curiously exotic, "un-English" elegance. Fritillaries have many associations with Oxford:

> I know what white, what purple fritillaries
> The grassy harvest of the river-fields
> Above by Ensham, down by Sandford, yields . . .

I wonder if the Fritillaries were sold, in Matthew Arnold's day, in the streets of Oxford, as they were in mine, and perhaps are still: the hawkers charged sixpence a bunch—it didn't seem much for these dusky, elegant gipsy-flowers, which seemed to have sprung, like Persephone herself, from some shadowy depth beneath the fields of Enna.

The Fritillary has taken us to the stream-side meadows, with their

> Lady-smocks all silver-white,
> And cuckoo-buds of yellow hue.

Shakespearian scholars seem to have cast no doubts on "lady-smocks," which are obviously *Cardamine pratensis*; the cuckoo-buds, however, are a famous stamping ground for pedants. My own view is that, by association with "lady-smocks," they are, without a doubt, Marsh Marigolds: I cannot imagine why anybody should suppose otherwise. However, the prefix "Cuckoo" is so universal among flower-names that one can never be sure. Lady's-smock itself is often called Cuckoo-flower, and has a good many other names as well; A. R. Horwood, in his *British Wild Flowers*, gives a list which includes the following: May Blob, Milk-girl, Paigle, Apple-pie, Canterbury Bells (!), Bird's-eye, Bogspinks, Bonny-bird-Een, Cuckoo's Head, Cuckoo-pint, Bread and Milk, Cuckoo's-shoes-and-stockings, Gookoo Buttons, Headache, Lady Flock, Lamb Lakins, Lucy Locket, Pigeon's Eye, Smell Smock, Whitsuntide, Gilliflower, Spink, etc., etc.

Cuckoo-flower is applied also to at least two of the orchids—*Orchis mascula* and *Orchis morio*. In the above list, Gookoo Buttons strikes me as a particularly pleasant variant. . . . Cuckoo-buds lead Shakespeare naturally enough—as they would have led any Elizabethan —to the cuckold joke. Why has this hoariest of old chestnuts entirely vanished from English popular life? The answer, I suppose, is (as so often) that the Puritans killed it; yet other bawdy old jokes have survived, in spite of the Noncomformist conscience. I don't know whether it has vanished in this way in other Protestant countries; it certainly hasn't from the Catholic ones—French and Italian comic papers are still full of "notable horns." I may have a primitive sense of humour, but I must confess that I like the cuckold joke—and the cruder it is the more I like it: those absurd Italian picture-postcards, for instance, in which the newly-married husband is shown sprouting a vast coiffure of antlers. . . . Perennially funny among Italian working-men, the joke is now only appreciated, in this country, by dons and "intellectuals"—surely an odd state of affairs.

The Marsh Marigold, *Caltha palustris* is the noblest of buttercups, and indeed has that aristocratic air which, in this country, one is apt to associate with rarity. Fritillary, Pasque Flower, Setterwort, Monkshood, Lady Orchid—these are all aristocrats, and all rare. Perhaps the mere fact of its rarity can make a plant seem distinguished, even if it's not; I doubt it, though—for some flowers, however rare, remain obstinately plebeian: *Cerastium pumilum*, for instance—a botanist's prize which none the less remains (for me at least) a mere Chickweed. Nor, though I'm particularly attached to the orchids, can I ever muster much enthusiasm for *Malaxis paludosa* or the Lesser Twayblade, rare though they are. No: I don't think rarity, alone, has much to do with it—and I would rather find the Marsh Marigold, any day, than the Bristol Rock-cress.

The Marigold is variable in its flowering season—Curtis records it, in 1775, as blooming in February; usually it will be out by early April, but may be later. Gerarde speaks of the "gallant green" leaves and "goodly yellow flowers, glittering like gold," which seems an adequate description. Oddly enough, this "herb of the sun" seems to have been credited with no medicinal virtues whatsoever.

By stream-sides, too, one may come across the Butterbur, a relation of the year's first flower, Winter Heliotrope. Butterbur is larger, with denser, more symmetrical flower-heads, and leaves which may be as much as a yard in diameter. The flowers are said to be particularly rich in honey, and I have read that bee-keepers in Sweden plant the Butterbur near their hives for this reason. Both Gerarde and Culpepper recommend a decoction of Butterbur for the plague, on account of its sudorific properties; it was also good for "spots and blemishes of the skin," a fact which provokes Culpepper into remarking, rather oddly, that "it were well if Gentlewomen would keep this Root preserved, to help their poor Neighbours. *It is fit the Rich should help the Poor, for the Poor cannot help themselves.*" One admires Culpepper's sentiments, of course, but one can't help feeling that "the poor" might have helped themselves to the extent of digging up a few Butterbur roots, without the assistance of their betters.

It is pleasant, by the way, to learn that Butterbur, in Curtis's day, grew "on the north side of the River Thames, betwixt *Westminster Bridge* and *Chelsea*"—whence, no doubt, the neighbouring "gentlewomen" procured their supplies; at least, one likes to think so, if only for the sake of the "poor" in those riverside districts which, already, must have foreshadowed the "rookeries" of the nineteenth century.

The first warm days, lethargic and unsettling, tempt one to sit in the garden; and at the seaside, somebody is sure to say "It's almost warm enough to bathe." More than any other month, April varies from year to year; nothing is ever certain, in the matter of English weather, but a fine, dry April is bound to make one dubious about the coming summer. One prefers to see

> skies of couple-colour as a brinded cow,

skies out of Constable's pictures; and one expects rain. Yet April is not really a very rainy month—August is apt to be wetter. Rain in England is an odd affair altogether: who would suppose that our climate was drier than Biarritz, Florence or Florida? Yet such, it seems, is the case, as my friend Stephen Bone has pointed out in his fascinating book, *British Weather*. The trouble is, we suffer from long spells of damp, grey days during which the actual rainfall is too slight to be recorded by the rain gauge; yet in retrospect it seems to have been "wet" all the time.

But April, the cruellest month, is (I still think) the loveliest: its finest days hold always the threat of winter's return; they are transitory, and therein lies their romantic charm. The wind backs round to the north again, sleet and hail ravage the wild cherry and flatten the spineless "All-bonie" in the hedges; the "blackthorn winter" returns, renewing with a colder whiteness the falling sloe-blossom. . . . But the sun comes out, the evening is suddenly warm, the thrushes sing:

> While still my temples ached from the cold burning
> Of hail and wind, and still the primroses
> Torn by the hail were covered up in it,
> The sun filled earth and heaven with a great light
> And a tenderness, almost warmth, where the hail dripped,
> As if the mighty sun wept tears of joy . . .[1]

> [1] Edward Thomas.

May

May is Mary's month and I
Muse at that and wonder why[1]

—but the Queen of Heaven has many names: she is Astarte, Cybele, Diana; and May, the month of summer's return, is her season. She presides over the May-day dances—

The association of man and woman
In daunsinge, signifying matrimonie

—and over the lighting of the Beltane fires; she is the May-Queen or May-lady, the Lady of the Trees; Artemis or Mary.

If one had to choose a single week out of all the year in which to be in England, I suppose one would decide on the first week of May: the true peak of the year, a climax more truly dramatic than midsummer itself; the season of

Growth in everything—

Flesh and fleece, fur and feather,
Grass and greenworld all together;
Star-eyed strawberry-breasted
Throstle above her nested

Cluster of bugle blue eggs thin
Forms and warms the life within;
And bird and blossom swell
In sod or sheath or shell . . .

[1] Hopkins: *The May Magnificat.*

71

Hopkins' vision is so fresh and so acute, yet at the same time so solid and "rooted," that he might be called the Cézanne of English poetry. Such comparisons are always dangerous and usually silly; but if Cézanne wanted to "do Poussin over again on Nature," one can imagine Hopkins feeling tempted to "do" Chaucer (and Langland) over again on the contemporary English scene. A Catholic and a Jesuit, Hopkins was the most profoundly English of modern poets—more so even than Edward Thomas.

Notice, by the way, those "bugle blue eggs" in the stanza quoted above: most poets would have been content with "sky-blue" or (at a stretch) speedwell- or even periwinkle-blue. Nobody but Hopkins would have thought of bugle, which is not a mere colour association but (using the word rather loosely) an "ecological" one: the eye falls from the nest in the hedge to the patch of bugle on the bank below.

Bugle was always one of my favourite flowers: true, it's not a very exciting or glamorous plant—it's not even "rare." But my affection for it was, so to say, comradely rather than amorous: one greeted it, each spring, as an old friend, plain, downright, dependable. . . . "Those that have Bugle and Sanicle need no surgeon," says Ray quoting an old French adage; its virtues were manifold, but it was chiefly a vulnerary herb, and was good for all wounds and sores, whether taken inwardly or applied to the place. Culpepper appears to have devoted particular attention to it:

"The Truth is, I have known this Herb cure some Diseases of *Saturn*, of which I thought good to quote one. Many times such as give themselves much to drinking are troubled with strange Fancies, strange Sights in the Night-time, and some with Voices, as also with the Disease *Ephialtes*, or the *Mare*. . . . These I have known cured by taking only two spoonfuls of the Syrup of this herb. . . . But whether this does it by Sympathy or Antipathy, is some doubt in Astrology. I know there is a great Antipathy between *Saturn* and *Venus* in matter of Procreation; yea, such a one that the Barrenness of *Saturn* can be

C*

removed by none but *Venus*; nor the Lust of *Venus* be repelled by none but *Saturn*, but I am not of opinion this is done this Way, and my Reason is, because these Vapours, though in Quality melancholy, yet by their flying upward, seem to be something Aerial; therefore I rather think it is done by Sympathy; *Saturn* being exalted in *Libra*, in the House of *Venus*."

Besides the name Bugle (says the same writer), the plant was also called Middle Consound, Middle Comfry, Brown Bugle, Sickle-wort and Herb Carpenter—though he adds that the last of these was, in Essex, applied to "another plant"—probably Self-heal, which rather resembles Bugle in appearance, and shared its repute as a "Wound Wort."

The four-square turrets of dull blue cover the ground in great patches: pleasant as Bugle is, one has to discourage it severely in the garden, where it spreads with an almost uncanny rapidity. Occasionally the flowers are pink or white: Ray found a red-flowered variety growing "plentifully in the second field on the left-hand going from Weston Green to Eltham." There are two other native "Bugles"—*Ajuga pyramidalis* and *Ajuga chamaepitys*, the first very, the second rather rare. *Ajuga chamaepitys*, the Ground Pine, is nothing like Bugle, having finely divided pine-like leaves and small yellow flowers. It is a haunter of dry banks and chalk-downs, chiefly in southern England.

It is the moment, in early to mid-May, when the

> azuring-over greybell makes
> Wood banks and brakes wash wet like lakes
> And magic cuckoo call
> Caps, clears, and clinches all . . .

We are past the magical first week of the month, the Bluebell is just past its prime—it has become, as Hopkins acutely observes, a "grey-bell." Among the "azuring-over" masses, are clumps of Wood Spurge and Red Campion: it is one of those floral "associations" which are as inevitable as bacon-and-eggs or whisky-and-soda. These ecological groupings of plants are fascinating, and particularly noticeable, I think, in this country. Elsewhere—in the Alps, in Italy—flowers seem more independent, less bound, as it were, by ecological "convention": the Lady Orchid, for instance, in Italy, will often enough escape from the copse where it belongs and pop up, unexpectedly, in the middle of a vineyard. In England, such unconventional behaviour is very unusual: flowers tend to remain in their normal situations, and to consort only with those others which share their "social background." Our native flowers, in fact, seem to reflect something of the complex, parochial structure of English society, and not a little of its snobbery: a Lady Orchid, in England, would never demean herself by "pigging it" in a mere cornfield—the very idea! Personally, I'm all in favour of this floral caste-system, and of the social groupings which evolve from it—for example, this May-time association of Bluebell, Campion and Wood Spurge.

> The wind flapped loose, the wind was still,
> Shaken out dead from tree and hill:
> I had walk'd on at the wind's will,—
> I sat now, for the wind was still . . .
>
> My eyes, wide open, had the run
> Of some ten weeds to fix upon;
> Among those few, out of the sun,
> The wood spurge flower'd, three cups in one . . .[1]

Euphorbia amygdaloides is the most attractive of the commoner spurges: some of the rarer ones—Caper Spurge, Portland Spurge—run it close, and I am fond, too, of the Cypress Spurge which, with its feathery leaves, doesn't look like a spurge at all. Wood Spurge is semi-evergreen, one can find its dark, purplish leaves all the year round, and the tall clusters of pale, milky-green flowers echo the young, fresh green of the hazels and hornbeams which form their background.

The Spurge family produces castor oil and tapioca—not much of a recommendation; all the spurges are poisonous, though many are of some commercial value—even the Manioc, says Miss Pratt, "affords

[1] Rossetti: *The Wood Spurge.*

in its root the nutritious Cassava, the bread made of which is by the Creoles preferred to that made of wheaten flour; and from the same root we derive the useful tapioca." (I like Miss Pratt's word "useful": it is tolerant though non-committal.) The Wood Spurge itself seems to have had no especial virtues—unlike the Sun Spurge, for instance, which was considered good for the bites of adders, or *Euphorbia coralloides*, said to be "extensively used by the peasantry of Kerry for stupefying fish." All the spurges secrete an acrid, milky juice, whose caustic properties vary with different species: the most potent appears to be the Sea Spurge, *Euphorbia paralias*, about which Gerarde speaks from personal experience: "Walking along the sea cost at Lee in Essex, with a gentleman called Master *Rich* dwelling in the same towne, I tooke but one drop of it into my mouth; which neverthelesse did so inflame and swell in my throte that I hardly escaped with my life: And in like case was the gentleman which caused us to take our horses, and poste for our lives unto the next farme house to drinke some milk to quench the extremitie of our heate, which then ceased."

One can't help being sorry for poor Master Rich, who must there-after have fought shy of visiting botanists; and even Gerarde himself, after this alarming experience, cannot bring himself to recommend the spurges with much enthusiasm: "These herbes by mine advise would not be received into the bodie, considering that there be so many other wholesome potions . . . that may be taken without perill, remembring the old worne proverbe, Deare is the honie that is lickt out of thornes. . . ."

> He is English as this gate, these flowers, this mire.
> And when at eight years old Lob-lie-by-the-fire
> Came in my books, this was the man I saw.
> He has been in England as long as dove and daw,
> Calling the wild cherry tree the merry tree,
> The rose campion Bridget in her bravery . . .[1]

[1] Edward Thomas: *Lob.*

The Campion is also known as Bachelors' Buttons, a name which it shares with several other plants. Erasmus Darwin, in that curious poem *The Loves of the Plants*, writes of it in terms which rather suggest Swinburne's "nymph in the brake":

> But when soft hours on breezy pinions move,
> And smiling May attunes her lute to love,
> Each wanton beauty, trick'd in all her grace,
> Shakes the bright dew-drops from her blushing face;
> In gay undress displays her rival charms,
> And calls her wondering lovers to her arms . . .

Bridget-in-her-bravery is, in fact, rather a prim-looking flower, and hardly suggests, by her appearance, that her love-life is so gay. More seductive, one would imagine, is the Wild Columbine, most elegant of all our wild flowers: the whole plant—leaves, stem and blossom—seems to me to have a perfectly proportioned, an almost classical beauty which has few rivals anywhere, and certainly none in England. Many people refuse to believe that the Columbine is really wild in this country; yet it is a true native, though like the daffodil somewhat "local," and apt to stray into (as much as out of) cultivation. As often as not, one finds it in small colonies, but occasionally (and this happens usually in open spaces in the woods, or in areas which have been recently coppiced) it is really abundant. It is then a magnificent sight: thousands upon thousands of the dusky violet flowers fluttering in the gentle May breeze, as though a swarm of some rare migrant butterfly had suddenly descended upon the land.

> Bring hether the Pincke and purple Cullambine,
>   With Gilliflowers;
> Bring Coronations, and Sops-in-wine
>   Worne of Paramoures,

wrote Spenser, though only the purple Columbine is considered truly wild—the "pincke" one is likely to be a garden-escape if one finds it in the woods. In the garden, the Columbine has been developed into an astonishing range of varieties and hybrids; gardeners snobbishly prefer the botanical name, Aquilegia, to the good old English Columbine, just as balletomanes prefer (or used to prefer in Diaghileff's day) Russian names for English dancers. . . . Both "Columbine" and "Aquilegia" refer to the shape of the flowers, which has suggested in the one case the form of a dove, in the other that of an eagle.

> This air breathed milky sweet
> With nodding columbine,
> Dangled upon the age-gnarled thorn
> The clematis twine . . .

As a matter of fact, I rather doubt if Walter de la Mare ever saw Columbines growing on the open downland (the poem is called *English Downs*); he might have found them in the beech-hangers, but I suspect that for him the name "Columbine" was on a par with Amaranth and Moly, Eglantine, Woodbine and all those other conventional and labour-saving flowers beloved by poets. (The glamour of Moly seems to me inexplicable—it is a kind of garlic, and I can't see Tennyson or anyone else lying on a bed of it for long.)

At school, I was always disappointed by the accredited "Nature Poets"—Wordsworth, Clare, W. H. Davies and the various Georgian "week-enders"; they so seldom wrote about flowers with real understanding, and even when they did they were too often inaccurate. The only poet in the whole of English literature who seemed to me to write both feelingly and knowledgeably about flowers was one (I had not yet discovered Hopkins) who wasn't considered a "Nature" poet at all—Matthew Arnold. *The Scholar Gypsy* and *Thyrsis* seemed to me then and seem still the best evocations of the English countryside ever written—not excepting Thomas and Hopkins.

One tends always to think of Arnold—at least, I do—in these "sweet spring days,"

> With whitening hedges, and uncrumpling fern,
> And blue-bells trembling by the forest-ways . . .

Arnold is pleasantly detached and commonsensical about his flowers; he never gushes over them; moreover, he calls them by their right names, and one feels that he had really seen them and knew where they grew. (He would never, like de la Mare, have written of columbines growing on chalk-hills.)

The "uncrumpling fern" would be mostly bracken in Oxfordshire, and no doubt Arnold was thinking of those curled, somehow heraldic-looking shoots which are shaped like the handle of a violin. They spring in their thousands among the bluebells and campion, and have a juicy, nourishing appearance which has led many people to eat them; they are, in fact, edible, but (from all accounts) rather nasty.

Here and there, among the bluebells and the overgrown Dog's Mercury, one will come upon patches of Herb-Paris—a rareish plant, but fairly abundant wherever it occurs. Its name has nothing to do with the French capital, but is derived from *par*, *paris*, equal, in reference to its symmetrical form. All parts of the plant are in fours, and this gives it a curiously prim, rather self-satisfied air: Herb-Paris is altogether too tidy and ship-shape to be a flower at all, and suggests more than anything else a proposition in Euclid; if it could speak, one feels, it would be able to say nothing more exhilarating than "Q.E.D." Like the Butcher's Broom, it is a sort of honorary member of the Lily family—in the sight of (botanical) man, that is to say; it could hardly be a lily in the sight of God. Its purple ovary (afterwards becoming a berry) stares balefully at one from the exact centre of all this geometrical perfection; one is almost relieved when one comes across (as one occasionally does) a "freak" with five leaves instead of the usual four.

Other names for Herb-Paris are One-berry and True-love; it is poisonous, causing convulsions and delirium when taken in large doses. None the less, Herb-Paris has been used in homeopathic medicine, and Gerarde recommends it, rather oddly, as an antidote "to repress the rage and force of poison." It was also good, he says, for "such as are become peevish, or without understanding"—possibly an early form of shock therapy.

79

One is always rather surprised, in reading old descriptions of May Day, by the fact that the weather seems always to have been warm and summer-like; the fact is, of course, that May the First fell a fortnight later according to the Old Calendar, which perhaps explains how the Hawthorn got its name of "May." Often it's not in full blossom, nowadays, till early June; though it ought to be out by mid-May, given a fairly mild spring.

Hawthorn, for me, though I love it, is inclined to pall rather quickly; its beauty is breath-taking, voluptuous, but I prefer the snowy candour of the Blackthorn. Hawthorn reminds me always of some very elaborate and expensive kind of confectionery; and as Proust remarks, in his famous description of the hedge at Tansonville, the pink variety, being coloured, was "consequently of a superior quality, by the æsthetic standards of Combray, to the 'plain,' if one was to judge by the scale of prices at the 'stores' in the square, or at Camus's, where the most expensive biscuits were those whose sugar was pink."[1]

The "flowering" trees—in the obvious sense of the term—are mostly in bloom before the Hawthorn; May is their month—Buck-thorn, Wayfaring Tree, Guelder Rose, Bird-cherry; and not only the "flowering" kinds, but the others: the loveliness of the young green lasts on into early June, but May is the great tree-month. Oak and Ash are the latest to come into leaf; the ash-buds have a sealed, unpromising look till the last moment, and their burgeoning is the more dramatic:

> May
> Mells blue and snow white through them, a fringe and fray
> Of greenery: it is old earth's groping towards the steep
> Heaven whom she childs us by.

The Ash, by the way, has always been endowed with potent magical properties: it appears to have been a rival, in this respect, to the Oak. "In England," writes Frazer, "children are sometimes passed through a cleft ash tree as a cure for rupture or rickets, and thenceforward a sympathetic connexion is supposed to exist between them and the

[1] *Swann's Way* (tr. C. K. Scott-Moncrieff).

tree." The mode of effecting the cure was to "split a young ash sapling longitudinally for a few feet and pass the child, naked, either three times or three times three through the fissure at sunrise."[1]

May brings an increasing glory to the water-meadows, where the "cuckoo-buds" still spread their prodigal gold over the grassy levels. By stream-sides, the Forget-me-not makes patches of clear, china blue—*Myosotis palustris*, of all the wild species the only one which looks like a "true" Forget-me-not; most of the others are smaller and more subdued in colour, and deserve their name of "Scorpion-grass." Comfrey belongs to the same family, the *Boraginaceae*, a tall, rank plant whose flowers, though pretty, seem disproportionately small. They are either purple or pale, creamy yellow: I don't know the reason for this variability, but it is probably a "soil variation," for one doesn't usually find the two kinds of Comfrey in the same place. A vulnerary herb, its earlier name was "Great Consound," and it was highly thought of by the herbalists. Gerarde recommends it particularly for the "paine in the backe, gotten by any violent motion, as wrastling, or overmuch use of women."

If one is lucky, one may find in marshy meadows this month a rather handsome orchid: *Orchis latifolia*, the earliest of the Marsh Orchids, a confused and confusing group whose complex inter-relationships can baffle the most painstaking and conscientious of botanists. In most nineteenth-century floras, only one Marsh Orchid is described, but this has now been split up into no less than seven species and a number of varieties and sub-species. The situation is further complicated by the fact that the Marsh Orchids form hybrids, not only between themselves, but with other orchises as well. The botanical amateur will do well to approach them cautiously—though he may easily be excused for lumping them recklessly together as "just Marsh Orchids." *Orchis latifolia* used to be called *Orchis incarnata*, a more descriptive name, since the flowers are of a clear flesh pink, quite

[1] *The Golden Bough*, p. 682–3 (abridged edition).

distinct from any other British species. The other common Marsh Orchid, *Orchis prætermissa* (so called because botanists managed to "overlook" it until recent days), may be in flower by the end of the month: its tall spikes of bright crimson-purple are more conspicuous than *Orchis latifolia*, and, at a distance, look like Purple Loosestrife. A private theory of mine is that *Orchis prætermissa* is the "long purples" of Shakespeare—

> That liberal shepherds give a grosser name,
> But our cold maids do dead-men's-fingers call them . . .

The name "long purples" is fitting enough (though applied also to the Loosestrife), and so is "dead-men's-fingers," which plainly refers to the palmate, finger-like roots. As for the "grosser names," I think Shakespeare was confusing his "long purples" with the round-tubered orchises, such as *Orchis mascula*, all of which were formerly called by names which derived, obviously, from the testicular shape of the tubers. "It hath gotten almost as many several Names attributed to the several Sorts of it," says Culpepper, "as would almost fill a Sheet of Paper; as Dog-stones, Goat-stones, Fool-stones, Fox-stones, Satirion, Cullians. . . ."

Leaving the aristocratic (if somewhat licentious) orchids for the time being, I must refer to the teeming hordes of *Umbelliferæ* which, in May, are coming into flower in such quantity that the botanist, unless a professional one (and a specialist at that), may well relinquish in despair the task of trying to identify them all. The commonest and most obvious (and one of the prettiest) is the Beaked Parsley, *Anthriscus sylvestris*, which I've already referred to: often called "Cow Parsley," it fills hedgerow, copse and orchard throughout May with its froth of feathery white blossom. Far less obvious is the Wood Sanicle, which at a first glance doesn't look like an Umbellifer at all: its umbels are small and globular, and borne in little clusters at the top of the stem. It is common in woods among the bluebells and campion, and at one time was famous for its "virtues." As a vulnerary herb, it shared the honours with Bugle, Self-heal and Comfrey; to-day it is not, so far as I know, used at all; but it is a pretty plant, and worth transplanting to the "wild" parts of a garden, where it thrives on the richer soil.

Another Umbellifer which needs no such encouragement is Gout-weed, *Ægopodium podagraria*, which, as Gerarde says, "groweth of itselfe in gardens, without setting or sowing, and is so fruitfull in his increase, that where it hath once taken roote, it will hardly be gotten out againe, spoiling and getting every yeere more ground, to the annoying of better herbes." It is edible, and can be cooked as a vegetable: Mr. Jason Hill, in his amusing little book on native foods,[1] says that it has a delicate flavour, "slightly reminiscent of parsley." Gardeners, he adds, "will eat it with vindictive satisfaction." Gastronomy quite apart, it is said to be good for gout (hence the name) and, as Culpepper says, for other "cold griefs"—a phrase which, to my mind, has an almost Mallarméan distinction. Other names for the plant are Bishop's Weed, Ground Elder and Herb Gerarde.

Another, more distinguished, Umbellifer is Samphire, *Crithmum maritimum*. It is one of those fleshy, glaucous, maritime plants which seem half-way to being seaweeds: its rather dirty-looking yellowish umbels are abundant on waste patches by the sea, often extending on to the foreshore itself. In Shakespeare's day—and in more recent times—it was gathered perilously from the sheer cliff-side. Presumably the demand exceeded the supply, for there is no need, to-day, to scale the cliffs in search of Samphire. Indeed, it seems to prefer the lower levels, and, if one looks over the edge of "Shakespeare's Cliff" (so called) at Dover, no Samphire is to be seen. I have not tried Samphire-pickle, though it is said to be good; the leaves can also be eaten raw, and have a slight resemblance to gherkins.

Commenting on the plant's Shakespearian associations, Anne Pratt records that, as lately as the early nineteenth century, it was gathered at Dover "by suspending a rope from the summit of the cliff, on which a man descended." In 1823, however, one of the local samphire-gatherers "was thus occupied, when the rope suddenly gave way, and

[1] *Wild Foods of Britain* (A. & C. Black, London).

he was dashed to the earth and died immediately." This man, adds Miss Pratt, "had pursued his dangerous occupation during the summers of forty years, and would often talk to visitors of Shakspere and King Lear, jocosely saying that he himself was king in that little domain, for none ventured to gather his samphire." One imagines that he must have been the last practitioner—or very nearly the last—of an ancient and honourable profession.

"Herbe Robert bringeth foorth slender, weake and brittle stalkes, somewhat hairie, and of a reddish colour, as are often-times the leaves also, which are jagged and deepely cut, like unto those of Chervile, of a most lothsome stinking smell. The flowers are of a most bright purple colour; which being past, there follow certaine small heads, with sharpe beakes or bils of birds: the root is very small and threddie."

Not everyone would agree with Gerarde about the "lothsome stinking smell" of Herb Robert: some people rather like it. Nor does the above description say enough about the plant's most attractive feature—the brilliant crimson, merging into almost scarlet, of the leaves in autumn. Herb Robert is altogether rather a seductive plant; the Geranium family all have a certain elegance—not least the Hemlock Stork's-bill, with its finely divided, hemlock-like leaves and long, beak-like seed-vessels. This, like the Herb Robert, is to be found now in hedges, though it is less common. The Mountain Crane's-bill, *Geranium pyrenaicum*, with pale violet flowers, is rather rare, but not by any means confined to mountains. *Geranium sanguineum*, the Bloody Crane's-bill, belies its name (in one sense of the word, at least), and is the handsomest British geranium, unless one excepts the Meadow Crane's-bill, *Geranium pratense*, common enough on roadsides and in meadows in some counties, but not (alas) in mine.

Mention of the Meadow Crane's-bill reminds me that I've said nothing about the May-time hayfields, now white with Ox-eye Daisies or burnished with the coppery red spikes of sorrel. Docks and sorrels—they are a squalid race, but the common Meadow Sorrel,

Rumex acetosa, forms one of those pleasant "associations" with other plants of which I've spoken before, and for which one can forgive it a good deal. A more rewarding inhabitant of the hayfield is *Lychnis flos-cuculi*, Ragged Robin, like a pink campion whose petals have been snipped to shreds with a pair of scissors. As its Latin name implies, it is another of those plants to which the name "Cuckoo-flower" has been applied for no better reason, apparently, than that they flower when the cuckoo is singing. Similarly, the Green-winged Orchis, another meadow plant, shares with *Orchis mascula* the name of "Cuckoos"; it is not unlike the Early Purple, but the sepals and petals converge to form a hood, which is veined, on the inside, with dull green. Among "liberal shepherds" it was known as Fool's-stones, presumably from some fancied resemblance of the flower to a fool's cap.

> Strike, churl; hurl, cheerless wind, then; heltering hail
> May's beauty massacre and wisped wild clouds grow
> Out on the giant air; tell Summer No,
> Bid joy back, have at the harvest, keep Hope pale.[1]

May seldom passes without one or two "throw-backs" to the previous month, or even to winter: the "heltering hail" flattens the hay harvest, the apple blossom is nipped ruinously by night-frosts; the last flowers of the cherry mingle their whiteness with the sudden powdering of hail at the wood's edge. More heart-breaking than the storms of April because less expected, a wet, cold May is the despair of farmers; and though it can be the loveliest of months, it can provoke one, more than most, into a hatred of one's own country. One thinks of the Tuscan spring, and is tempted to explain the English temperament in terms of English weather: frost-in-May is the very climate of Puritanism—"bid joy back, have at the harvest, keep Hope pale. . . ." Can one wonder, in such weather, at the Nonconformist Conscience?

[1] Hopkins.

June

So, some tempestuous morn in early June,
  When the year's primal burst of bloom is o'er,
    Before the roses and the longest day—
  When garden-walks and all the grassy floor
    With blossoms red and white of fallen May
And chestnut flowers are strewn—
  So have I heard the cuckoo's parting cry,
    From the wet field, through the vext garden-trees,
    Come with the volleying rain and tossing breeze:
  The bloom is gone, and with the bloom go I!

THE gales of May, the "heltering hail" even, can last well into June; swaddled in mackintoshes, cowering beneath umbrellas, we pretend that summer has come, and even (I suppose) extract a kind of snobbish satisfaction from our wretchedness. "This English climate," we mutter, and smile significantly, almost complicitly, one to another, tacitly implying that we wouldn't really exchange it for any other, and feeling that, since it's unpleasant, it must, in some mysterious way, be good for us. . . . No wonder we are Puritans; did the climate of northern Europe really begin to change for the worse about the time of the Reformation? It is a tempting theory, but one which must, I suppose, remain unproven for lack of evidence.

It may be a purely subjective impression on my part, but I invariably associate these days of late May and early June with rain; perhaps it is merely the effect of Arnold and Housman. But whatever the weather may do, this season is, in a sense, a "little autumn," the "primal burst of bloom" is over, and there is, as it were, a lull "before the roses and the longest day."

86

June, of course, can be hopelessly wet and bleak, from beginning to end—who will ever forget that desolate, heart-breaking summer of 1946? Yet in a good—even an "average"—year, it is the loveliest of months, justifying all that has ever been said or sung about it, from Shakespeare and Hopkins down to the latest dance-lyric. And even a wet June won't stop the flowers from coming out—though it may delay them.

> Too quick despairer, wherefore wilt thou go?
> Soon will the high Midsummer pomps come on,
>   Soon will the musk carnations break and swell,
> Soon shall we have gold-dusted snapdragon,
>   Sweet-William with his homely cottage-smell,
> And stocks in fragrant blow . . .

Among the "pomps" of midsummer (garden flowers quite apart) I suppose the common Corn Poppy must take pride of place. It is one of the three *scarlet* flowers found wild in this country—the other two are Scarlet Pimpernel and the Pheasant's Eye, *Adonis annua*. All three can be found in cornfields, though *Adonis* is rare. (The only other native plant which can fairly be called "scarlet" is a rare variety of Marsh Orchid, *Orchis latifolia* var. *coccinea*; this, however, is more of a light vermilion than true scarlet, and is, moreover, a very local plant, occurring only in a few bogs in Wales.) Pheasant's Eye is a charming anemone, with finely-divided, fern-like leaves, and small flowers which look like drops of arterial blood spilt among the bright green foliage. If it grows among poppies (as it often does) the more modest charms of *Adonis* are apt to be passed over.

> Summer set lip to earth's bosom bare,
> And left the flushed print in a poppy there:
> Like a yawn of fire from the grass it came,
> And the fanning wind puffed it to flapping flame . . .

"A yawn of fire"—the poppy inevitably breeds these somnolent images. "Not poppy nor mandragora." . . . But the English Corn Poppy has never, I think, been extensively used as an opiate. In the poem I've quoted, Francis Thompson describes it further as

> lethargied with fierce bliss,
> And hot as a swinkèd gipsy is,
> And drowsed in sleepy savageries.

A country name for the poppy is "Headaches," and for me the plant evokes always a particular complex of associations: hot, "headachy" afternoons of midsummer, haunted by a vague, post-prandial malaise, and throbbing with the insistent drone of an aeroplane high in the blue, like the external echo of a migraine. . . . The poppy is at its best, I think, in early June, when its first "yawn of fire" breathes through the young green corn—a moment which Hopkins captured in his fragmentary, unfinished poem, *The Woodlark*:

> The blue wheat-acre is underneath
> And the braided ear breaks out of the sheath,
> The ear in milk, lush the sash,
> And crush-silk poppies aflash,
> The blood-gush blade-gash
> Flame-rash rudred
> Bud shelling or broad-shed
> Tatter-tassel-tangled and dingle-a-dangled
> Dandy-hung dainty head . . .

One is almost glad *The Woodlark* was never finished: in no other poem that I know does one have so vivid a sense of actually assisting at the act of creation—the phrases come spilling out one after another, half formulated yet astonishingly vivid; the effect is of some brilliant lightning sketch by a great painter, executed on the back of an envelope to amuse a child. "Crush-silk"—the phrase flashes out, exact and inevitable, to describe the opening poppy-bud, with its crumpled petals swelling forth like bundles of silk squashed together in a too small bag. And "blood-gush blade-gash"—the very first buds to open, blobs of scarlet, startling as a hæmorrhage among the young green.

"In classic lore," says Sowerby, "the Corn Poppy has long been held sacred to Ceres; as it is, however, by no means a welcome guest in the fields dedicated to her service, we may regard it rather as a sacrifice required by her from her worshippers, than as an offering to be encouraged. . . ."[1]

The poppy, in other words, is a pest—and one which shows no signs of diminishing, in spite of the considerable advances which have been made, in recent years, in the purifying of imported grain. It is a technical triumph which, though a boon to farmers, must be regretted by the botanist; for a number of cornfield "weeds," once very common, have nowadays become rare. The poppy has resisted all such attempts at "liquidation," and I cannot say I am sorry; the blue Cornflower, on the other hand, is now so scarce that it can scarcely be counted as a British plant at all. I have found it wild on one occasion only—and that was many years ago; moreover, I found only a single plant, and that may well have been an "escape." Yet in almost any nineteenth-century flora the Cornflower is described as a common British wild flower. "A common weed in cornfields," says Sowerby,[2] and if one was brought up, as I was, on Victorian flower books, one continues to associate the Cornflower, inevitably, with the poppies and wheat-ears among which it figured in so many colour prints of wild "nosegays." Perhaps I'm wrong about the Cornflower— possibly it may still be common in some parts of the country; I can only say that I have failed, for the last thirty years or so, to come across it. What makes its rarity even more extraordinary is that in northern France, all along the Channel coast, it is still extremely abundant, and is one of the first wild flowers one notices as one's train pulls out of Calais.

Another cornfield plant which I used to find in my childhood, but which I have not seen since, is the Corncockle: perhaps it was never as common as the Cornflower, in which case its disappearance is less surprising. But the passing of both these "weeds" is to be regretted. Even the Corn Marigold, though still common enough in some districts, is less abundant than formerly: it is almost absent from Kent, though that is probably because it doesn't thrive well on chalk.

[1] *English Botany* (1873 edition).　　　[2] Ibid (1799 edition).

There are still, however, a number of cornfield plants which have resisted all efforts to extirpate them—the Fumitory, for example, though even this has changed in quality if not in quantity in recent years: one of the two common species seems to have increased, for no obvious reason, at the other's expense. Fumitory is one of those not very noticeable plants which (like Milkwort and Sanicle) seem to have acquired a disproportionate reputation in medicine and magic. It is also an exceedingly "literary" plant: one could compile, I suppose, quite an extensive anthology of poetic and other allusions to it. Shakespeare himself seems to have had a fondness for Fumitory: I can think of two references right away—in *Lear* and *Henry V*—and there are probably more. Clare refers, rather sceptically, to its use as an anti-sunburn lotion:

> And fumitory too,—a name
> That superstition holds to fame—
> Whose red and purple-mottled flowers
> Are cropped by maids in weeding hours,
> To boil in water, milk, and whey,
> For washes on a holiday,
> To make their beauty fair and sleek,
> And scare the tan from Summer's cheek . . .

According to Burton, it was "not to be omitted by those who are misaffected" with melancholy—rather a negative recommendation, but one which is backed up by Culpepper, who also prescribes it for "Madness, Forgetfulness, Jaundice, yellow and black," as well as for the Plague, "being taken with good Treacle." In a fourteenth-century manuscript "secured" (according to Sowerby)[1] "by T. J. Pettigrew from the Royal Library at Stockholm," a certain John of Milan praises the "fumiter" as a febrifuge:

> *Fumiter* is erbe, I say,
> Yt springyth i April et in May,
> In feld, in town, in yard, et gate,
> Where lond is fat and good in state.

[1] *English Botany* (1873 edition).

Dun red is his flour,
Ye erbe smoke lik in colowur,
Ageyn feuerys cotidian,
And ageyn feuerys tertyen,
And ageyn feuerys quartyn
It is medicyn souereyn.

The name "fumitory" seems to have puzzled botanists unduly—
myself, I cannot see the difficulty. "This plant," says Sowerby,[1] "is
called in some old books *Fumus terrae* (smoke of the earth), a name
perhaps more intelligible to the sapient writers than to us." I shouldn't
have thought one had to be very "sapient" to see why the

lace-leaved lovely
Foam-tuft fumitory[2]

was called "Earth-smoke": the grey-green, feathery foliage suggests
precisely a drift of smoke creeping between the furrows. Sowerby,
one suspects, was (like a good many professional botanists) too
academic by half, despite his ironic disclaimer.

The numerous tribe of Mayweeds—stinking, scentless and the rest—
are apt to prove baffling to all but specialists; as a child, I regarded
them all as "Chamomile"—I suppose somebody had told me that that
was their name. (Chamomile itself, an allied plant, is in fact rather
rare). Other cornfield "weeds" worth a glance are the Wild Pansy,
or Heartsease, and the Charlock. The latter is at its best when it
occupies the whole field—particularly when the next field is full of
poppies; the contrast of yellow and scarlet is breath-taking. The
Heartsease is (I have always thought) rather disappointing—it has the
air of a violet masquerading, rather unsuccessfully, as a pansy. Herrick's
poem seems to me an undeserved compliment:

Frollick Virgins once there were,
Overloving, (living here):
Being here their ends deny'd
Ran for sweethearts mad, and dy'd.

[1] *English Botany* (1799 edition).   [2] Hopkins: *The Woodlark*.

Love in pitie of their teares,
And their losse in blooming yeares,
For their restlesse here-spent-houres,
Gave them *Hearts-ease* turn'd to flowers.

I am fonder of the pink Convolvulus, which has acquired no such aura of sentiment, and has no medicinal virtues: Gerarde calls it an "unprofitable weede," and it is a nuisance to the farmer, but an elegant and charming plant for all that. Another cornfield nuisance is the Knot-grass, which nobody could call attractive: I mention it only because, squalid and insignificant as it is, it has been honoured (for some mysterious reason) by no less a person than W. B. Yeats:

He mused beside the well of Scanavin,
He mused upon his mockers: without fail
His sudden vengeance were a country tale,
When earthly might had drunk his body in;
But one small Knot-grass growing by the pool
Sang where—unnecessary cruel voice—
Old silence bids its chosen race rejoice . . .[1]

Has Knot-grass any particular significance in Celtic mythology? I don't know; but I can't imagine that Yeats mentioned it merely for its own sake, or because he liked it. Even the herbalists are not particularly enthusiastic about the Knot-grass—the best that Gerarde, for instance, can find to say in its favour, is that it is effective, "being shred and made in a tansie with egs," against gonorrhœa.

A month ago one still had to "look for" flowers—in the woods, in meadows, by the streamside; by mid-June, there is no escaping them, and if one is catholic enough in one's tastes, one can botanize as happily on a blitzed site or suburban rubbish-tip as at Teesdale or the Lizard. A surprising number of plants belong to the category known as "viatical": one never finds them far from man's footsteps. In many cases they are, of course, "aliens" or garden escapes; but by no means always. The *Umbelliferæ* and *Cruciferæ* seem particularly fond of

[1] *The Man who Dreamed of Faeryland.*

roadsides, and so do the Composites. A border-line case—often found on rubbish-heaps and by roadsides, yet possibly indigenous—is the Borage. Its brilliant, gentian-blue flowers, with their black, spiky centres, are very lovely, though the plant as a whole has a rather coarse, plebeian appearance. The seductive sprig of borage which floats in a jug of claret cup is, I suppose, a survival from the days when the plant was genuinely used as a "cooling" drink. It seems, moreover, to have had anti-melancholic virtues as well: "the leaves, flowers and seede," says Parkinson, "all of them, or any of them, are very cordiall, and helpe to expell pensiveness and melancholy, that ariseth without manifest cause, whereof came the saying—

Ego Borrago gaudia semper ago!"

There was little to choose, for that matter, between Borage and the various kinds of Bugloss: all, according to Culpepper, were good for "putrid and pestilential fevers," and were held to benefit those who were "troubled with often swoonings, or Passions of the heart." Since Borage was usually, for medicinal purposes, infused in wine, one can't help suspecting that its role as a "cordiall" was a minor or (as the doctors say) an "adjuvant" one.

I have mentioned the Meadow Crane's-bill, *Geranium pratense*, before: it is as much a viatical as a meadow-growing plant, and I have seen it fringing the roads for miles in Berkshire and Oxfordshire. Many of its family share its taste for roadsides; so, too, do the *Solanaceæ*, the family of the Nightshades. Deadly as some of these are, the potato and tomato are both *Solanums*, and the potato plant is said to be poisonous above ground; so are the tubers themselves, if they are allowed to turn green.

The name "Nightshade" has acquired an almost mythical potency in the public mind, an atmosphere of Gothic horror which it is exceedingly difficult to dispel. Most people, for instance, cannot dissociate "Nightshade" from the epithet "deadly": all nightshades must *ipso facto* be Deadly Nightshade. This leads to endless confusion: a few years ago, an outbreak of poisoning cases occurred among children who were reported to have eaten "Deadly Nightshade" berries. The newspapers duly "wrote up" the affair with a great show of authority, illustrating their accounts with pictures of the lethal plant. Scarcely a single one of these reports took the trouble to be accurate: some described the Woody Nightshade, *Solanum dulcamara*, under the title of "Deadly Nightshade"; others described the true Deadly Nightshade, *Atropa belladonna*, and accompanied it by a picture of the Woody species; yet others printed a drawing of *Solanum* with the title of "Belladonna," and described its berries as black instead of red—and so on. So far as one could gather, the plant in question was either the Woody or the Black Nightshade—both poisonous, but variable in their effects: the toxicity of the berries is said to vary according to season. The true Deadly Nightshade was unlikely to have been the culprit, for it is (perhaps fortunately) a rather rare plant, confined mainly to chalk and limestone districts in the south.

So much for the freedom of the Press. More accurate than the modern journalist, Gerarde relates a story of Deadly Nightshade poisoning which does, genuinely, refer to *Atropa belladonna*: "It came to passe" (he says) "that three boies of Wisbich in the Ile of Ely, did eate of the pleasant and beautifull fruite heerof, two whereof died in lesse than 8 howers after they had eaten of them. The thirde childe had a quantitie of honie and water mixed togither given him to drinke, causing him to vomit often: God blessed the meanes and the child recovered." Gerarde adds a note of warning "to deale not . . . with a plant so furious and deadly," and especially to banish it from such places as "children or women with childe do resort, which do often-times long and lust after things most vile and filthie. . . ." None the less, as lately as 1799, Sowerby remarks that the leaves "given internally in infusion," were supposed to relieve the pain of cancer; though he adds that "the sufferings of the patient . . . were dreadful."

Atropa is not easily confused with the other nightshades: its broad, egg-shaped leaves are unmistakable, and still more so are the large flowers, the shape of Canterbury Bells, but of a curiously lurid brownish-purple, suggesting the colour of contused flesh. Woody

Nightshade, or Bittersweet, is common in hedges—a trailing, untidy plant with small purple flowers like those of the potato. Black Nightshade, similar but smaller, with white flowers (the name refers to the berries), is a common garden weed: it is more poisonous than Bittersweet, but by no means so "furious and deadly" as Belladonna— though, according to Curtis (*Flora Londiniensis*), it was "very powerful in its operation; even so small a quantity as one grain weight of the leaf . . . would sometimes produce a very considerable effect."

Also of the Nightshade family, and of a viatical tendency, are Thorn-apple and Henbane. Thorn-apple, *Datura stramonium*, is an exotic-looking plant suggesting, by its large, white, trumpet-shaped flowers, those tropical Daturas of which it is a near relation. Thorn-apple itself is an "introduced species," but, unlike most such "aliens," its naturalization papers are, so to speak, in order—we know almost exactly when it was introduced, and by whom: Gerarde tells us that he received the seeds "of the Right Honourable the Lord *Edward Zouch*, which he brought from Constantinople, and of his liberalitie did bestowe them upon me . . . and is that Thorn-apple that I have dispersed through this land. . . ."

The whole plant is poisonous; the drug stramonium is derived from it, but the use of Thorn-apple in herbal medicine was apt to be attended with disaster: "the plant is sometimes smoked in a pipe, to relieve asthma," says Miss Pratt, who goes on to add, in her usual cheerful way, that "convulsions have been caused by this practice."

Thorn-apple has never become very common: it is one of those plants which have remained "sporadic," as botanists say, turning up now here, now there, on rubbish heaps, by roadsides and in gardens. According to Curtis (1799) it was "found occasionally in the environs of London, on dung-hills, in cultivated ground and amongst rubbish."

Sporadic, too, is the Henbane, though it is sometimes very abundant where it occurs. I have seen a whole hillside, near Folkestone, almost covered with it; often, however, such colonies disappear, inexplicably, after a year or two, never to be re-established. Henbane is a sinister yet fascinating plant: its clammy, evil-smelling leaves would be enough to give it a bad reputation, quite apart from the flowers which, with their purple centres and intricately-veined petals, have an unhealthy, etiolated look which suggests that they have been grown in a cellar. The plant, one feels, was probably common in the neighbourhood of Udolpho or on the slopes of the Brocken; whether it was the "Hebanon" of *Hamlet* remains a matter for debate, but if it wasn't, it certainly ought to have been.

Like the Thorn-apple, Henbane yields a useful drug, hyoscine; and Maund, in his *Botanic Garden* (1834), remarks that it was sometimes smoked "in the manner of tobacco," to relieve toothache, though it appears to have been, like the Thorn-apple, of dubious value as an analgesic, "convulsions and temporary insanity" being the usual outcome. "The seede," says Gerarde, "is used of mountibancke tooth-drawers which runne about the countrey, for to cause woormes come foorth of mens teeth by burning it in a chafing dish with coles, the partie holding his mouth over the fume thereof: but some craftie companions to gaine money convey small lute strings into the water, perswading the patient that those small creeping beasts came out of his mouth or other parts. . . ."[1]

June is the month of roses, and it would be churlish not to mention them; yet, much as I like them for themselves and in the mass, they are apt to reduce me, as an amateur botanist, to a state of alarm and despondency. I'm not sure just how many subspecies and varieties are now included under *Rosa canina*; but they probably, by this time, run into three figures. I find the Dog-rose a charming flower, and like to see it sprawling waywardly over the midsummer hedges; but I'm ashamed to say that it remains for me a mere Dog-rose, as *Primula vulgaris* remained a yellow primrose for Peter Bell. There is *Rosa arvensis*, certainly, which is fairly easy to distinguish, and of course Sweet Brier and the pretty little Burnet Rose. Perhaps I have a "blind

[1] Several correspondents have informed me that this treatment is actually still in use; if so, one can only suppose that the "craftie companions," mentioned by Gerarde, are still assisting at the operation.

spot" about the genus; in the company of other botanists I am constantly being humiliated by my ignorance, just as, in literary circles, I suffer from a chronic sense of inferiority about the novels of Henry James. I know James is a master of the Art of Fiction; critics for whom I have a boundless respect have assured me of the fact; yet I continue to find him totally unreadable. I shall never, I know, manage to get through *The Ambassadors*; nor shall I ever succeed, alas, in distinguishing one variety of Dog-rose from another.

I am, on the other hand, fond of the Elder—an unpopular shrub, especially with gardeners. It must be the hardiest and toughest of all British plants—putting forth its leaves in mid-winter, and resisting every attempt to extirpate it: cut it down as often as you will, the juicy, brittle saplings will be breast-high again in a week or two. Yet in the flowering season, the big white plates of blossom cover this ignoble bush with a brief but transcendent glory. Not many people, I suppose, bother to make elderberry-wine nowadays; fewer still, presumably, gather the young shoots as a substitute for asparagus—though Culpepper recommends them as a corrective for "Phlegm and Choler."

Elder is one of several trees upon which Judas Iscariot is traditionally supposed to have hanged himself:

> Judas he japed
> With Jewen silver,
> And sithen on an eller
> Hanged hymselve.

One would suppose that the Fig-tree had a better claim than the Elder, which doesn't, usually, attain to a suitable size or strength for such a purpose. The association seems, in fact, pointless; and oddly enough the Dwarf Elder, *Sambucus ebulus*, a much more local plant, has attracted to itself an equally improbable legend—like the Pasque Flower, it is supposed to have sprung from the spilt blood of the Danish invader, though there is nothing in the least sanguinary about its appearance.

The hedgerows now, at midsummer, display a bewildering variety of plants—so much so, that one is compelled to be ruthlessly selective in describing them. Numerous vetches—the common *Vicia sativa*, with its small crimson flowers, is not the least attractive; Yellow Vetchling with its conspicuous yellow clusters is common too, and so is the handsome Tufted Vetch, *Vicia cracca*, with tall, erect spikes of violet blossom. The Wood Vetch, *Vicia sylvatica*, is rather rare: a handsome trailing plant whose white flowers are delicately veined with purple. Also rareish is the extraordinary Grass Pea, *Lathyrus nissolia*, indistinguishable, unless in flower, from the grasses among which it grows: the bright crimson blossoms appear mysteriously in the angles of the grass-like leaves, giving the plant an air of unreality—rather as though a child had amused himself by sticking vetch flowers among the grass blades. (I once, at my prep. school, played a similar trick on one of the mistresses, who professed to an interest in botany: attaching, in this case, the yellow flowers of Bird's-foot Trefoil to a withered spike of Self-heal; the lady was duly taken in, but not for long.)

The Bedstraws are another family about which I cannot feel very much enthusiasm: commonest (and least attractive) is the Goose-grass, or Cleavers, whose capacity for clinging is not atoned for by any compensatory charms—in which it resembles an extensive category of the human species. The masses of Lady's Bedstraw, clothing dry banks with fine-spun gold, are a pleasant sight; of the white-flowered Hedge Bedstraw, the best thing I can find to say is that it is the "host" of an interesting parasite, the Clove-scented Broomrape, *Orobanche caryophyllacea*. Rarest and most rewarding of the group, this Broomrape is confined to one or two localities in Kent; it is entirely dependent on the Bedstraw, its host; its chosen habitats, moreover, are in most cases easily accessible, and liable to be trodden over by trippers and golfers. Yet the Broomrape survives with an extraordinary tenacity: it can still be found, for instance, in at least one of the localities recorded by G. E. Smith in 1829.[1] *Orobanche caryophyllacea* is the most pleasing of

[1] G. E. Smith: *A catalogue of Rare or Remarkable Phænogamous Plants collected in South Kent* (London, 1829).

its genus: less "dead-looking" than the rest, varying in colour from creamy yellow to vivid purple, and remarkable for its strong scent of cloves.

Like the Roses, the *Umbelliferæ* are apt to induce, in the botanical amateur, a sense of guilt and inferiority: there are so many of them so much alike that one despairs of ever identifying them all. . . . In this context, however, I have a good excuse for being (as I intend to be) recklessly exclusive; and I propose to single out two only of this worrying family for special mention this month. The first is Hemlock—*Conium maculatum*, the "true" Hemlock, traditionally supposed to be the plant by which Socrates met his death, though the tradition cannot, I think, be taken very seriously. . . . Hemlock is a tall-growing plant (as much as six feet) with finely divided, fern-like foliage, and comparatively small umbels of white flowers; its most recognizable feature, however, is the stem, which is thickly dotted and stippled with purple—hence the Latin specific name. One cannot call the Hemlock a rarity, but it is local in its distribution, and seems to be nearly or quite absent from many districts. I have already mentioned Beaked Parsley, that commonest of hedgerow weeds, and I referred, I think, to the fact that, while its leaves are edible, the root is said to be poisonous. In the case of Hemlock, the situation is exactly reversed: above ground, the whole plant is virulently poisonous, but the root is said to be harmless. Woodville, in his *Medical Botany*, quotes Ray as saying "that the skilful herbalist, Mr. Petiver, ate half an ounce of the root of Hemlock, and that Mr. Henly, in the presence of Mr. Petiver, swallowed three or four ounces, without experiencing any remarkable effect." Woodville adds the further testimony (quoted from Curtis) of a Mr. T. Lane, who "also, with great caution, made some experiments of the like kind, and in a short time found he could eat a considerable part of the root, without any inconvenience . . . and found them as agreeable eating at dinner with meat as carrots, which they in taste somewhat resembled."

Personally, not being over-fond of carrots, I should hardly find it worth while to use Hemlock as a substitute for them; and would prefer to make a meal off Fennel, my second umbelliferous choice for this month. I believe that the *finocchi* of Italy are not quite the same as our wild *Fœniculum vulgare*, but they would be easy enough to cultivate in this country if we had not lost our taste for them. Fennel was still used, not so long ago, as a sauce for fish; nowadays, however, *finocchi* are only to be found (so far as this country is concerned) in Soho, and not always there.

Wild Fennel is found most often on sea-cliffs: its fine, feathery foliage resembles that of asparagus, and sets off pleasantly enough the umbels of yellow flowers. Its ancient reputation was not, apparently, confined to cookery:

> It gave new strength and fearless mood,
> And gladiators fierce and rude
> Mingled it in their daily food;
> And he who battled and subdued,
> The wreath of Fennel bore.[1]

It was included also (as Anne Pratt points out) among the plants "commonly strewed over the pathway of the newly married persons":

> The healthful balm and mint from their full laps do fly,
> The scentful camomile, the verdrous costmary.
> They hot muscado oil, with milder maudlin cast,
> Strong tansy, fennel cool, they prodigally waste . . .[2]

The roots, said Parkinson, were "used in broths, and the leaves more seldome, yet they serve to trimme up many fish meates"; and the seeds, apparently, were "much used to put in Pippin pies, and divers other such baked fruits, as also unto bread, to give it a better relish."

Speaking of edible plants reminds me of the wild Strawberry, which (like the Fennel) is not as much eaten in this country as it

[1] Longfellow.   [2] Drayton.

deserves to be. The only reason for this seems to be that we are just too lazy to gather it. Wild Strawberries, I admit, are irritating things to pick: but how rewarding they are—especially if steeped (as the custom is in France and Italy) in a glass of red or white wine. I suppose it was our former prosperity which destroyed our taste for such native delicacies: it was easier to buy cultivated strawberries than to go out and pick wild ones. Yet we still gather blackberries—a much inferior fruit. The Italian peasants, who will eat almost any wild herb or berry that is not downright poisonous, regard the blackberry as inedible. An Italian friend of mine, who keeps a *pensione* in the Abruzzi, told me that one of his guests, an old English lady, nearly caused a village scandal by her fondness for this fruit. The peasants, seeing her gathering blackberries in the hedges, concluded that the guests at the *pensione* must be starving. . . .

The Strawberry is one of those plants which, as Gilbert White pointed out,[1] has the habit of lying dormant for many years when conditions are unsuitable for it: "When old beech trees are cleared away, the naked ground in a year or two becomes covered with strawberry plants, the seeds of which must have lain in the ground for an age at least. One of the slidders or trenches down the middle of the Hanger, close covered over with lofty beeches near a century old, is still called strawberry slidder, though no strawberries have grown there in the memory of man." (I can remember, myself, a hill not far from Selborne called "Strawberry Hanger," but I don't think it was particularly notable for strawberries.)

In the woods, by mid-June, the later spring flowers—Bluebell, Campion, Bugle—are going over, elbowed aside by the more tawdry blossoms of summer: Foxglove, Golden Rod, St. John's Wort and the ubiquitous Rosebay Willowherb. From this category I must exclude Self-heal, a pleasant plant rather similar to Bugle, which it now replaces; they are so similar, indeed, that they were often confused by older writers: one finds such names as Sicklewort, Herb

[1] *Natural History of Selborne.*

Carpenter, etc., applied to both. Self-heal, like the Bugle, was a vulnerary herb, and guaranteed to cure any wound; its use in first-aid must, however, have been attended with some difficulty, for the leaves are small, and it would take a considerable time to gather sufficient quantity to stop even a minor hæmorrhage.

Foxglove is a noble plant, and very common in some districts, though in my own county it is rather scarce. Digitalin, so useful in cardiac conditions, is extracted from it; yet the Foxglove, though widely used in herbal medicine, seems formerly to have been esteemed chiefly for quite other diseases: Culpepper recommends it particularly for "a scabby head," and it was one of innumerable herbs which could be used at a pinch (and in default of the royal touch) against the King's Evil.

Rosebay Willowherb is, I suppose, known to everybody nowadays, since it is as much at home in Cheapside or the Tottenham Court Road as in the remotest corners of Dartmoor. Like the "Oxford" Ragwort, *Senecio squalidus*, it received a new lease of life during the blitz; for both these plants thrive on ground which has been recently scorched. Rosebay was always to be found where heath fires had occurred, and Oxford Ragwort came originally, I believe, from the slopes of Mount Etna. Both were rare plants a century ago: the Ragwort, an alien, was first established in the Oxford Botanic Gardens, whence it spread rapidly to the walls of the colleges and waste patches near the town; Rosebay appears to be indigenous, but as lately as the sixties was, as Anne Pratt remarks, "a rare plant in moist woods."

We have become blasé about the Willowherb nowadays, but it is a beautiful plant, especially when it first comes into flower: later, it has a rather blowsy air, due to the scruffy masses of pappus which clothe the lower part of the spike. It seems to be chiefly a plant of northern Europe, and is rare in Italy: the most impressive colony of Rosebay I ever encountered was half-way up an Italian mountain-side, where it acquired a kind of romantic glamour as much from its scarcity as from its surroundings. The friend with whom I was staying (the same who was reputed to "starve" his English guests) was also a botanist: he had never before seen the Rosebay, and was vastly impressed. I rather shocked him by bursting into irreverent laughter: it was odd to see such homage accorded to the "Fireweed" of our London blitzed sites. Yet within a few yards of the Rosebay were growing innumerable specimens of *Cephalanthera rubra*, the Red Helleborine—one of the rarest of British Orchids, which I had sought for in vain, in Gloucestershire, the year before. But my Italian friend was not in the least interested in the orchid which, to him, was a mere weed. . . .

Rosebay, says Sowerby,[1] is "one of those plants whose leaves are found in English adulterations of tea"—though I have not heard that the London "blitz-weed" has been used of late to spin out the post-war ration. Sowerby adds that the leaves also "form a wholesome vegetable when boiled," and that "the Kamschatkans make a kind of beer from the young shoots and the pith" which, added to *Agaricus muscarius*, is used "for the purpose of intoxication." But we are, as I have observed before, an unenterprising race: here is a plant which provides tea, beer and "greens," free, gratis and for nothing; yet we leave it unharvested. . . . They order these things better in Kamschatka.

There are many species of St. John's Wort—the most impressive is certainly the Rose of Sharon, whose big, golden flowers adorn plantations and shrubberies; but it is not truly wild. The commonest of the native species is *Hypericum perforatum*—the specific name refers to the translucent dots upon the leaves. In Wales it is called, for the same reason, "Thousand Holes," and also "y Fendigedi," the blessed—for St. John's Wort is a holy herb, sovereign against witchcraft. Why it was ever associated with St. John I don't know: but it was certainly used in the ceremonies of Midsummer Eve. It is another of those mysterious plants which have acquired a vast reputation in magic and medicine for no very obvious reason. J. E. Smith[2] remarks that "as this plant was found to bleed at the slightest touch, it was supposed to

[1] *English Botany* (1873 edition).
[2] Sir J. E. Smith: *The English Flora*, Vol. III (1829).

have a vulnerary quality, and became 'the balm of the warrior's wound.'" Woodville, in his *Medical Botany*, tells us further that it was "in great request with the ancients, who prescribed it in hysteria, hypochondriasis and mania. They also imagined that it had the peculiar power of curing demoniacs, and it thence obtained the name of *Fuga daemonum*."

All the St. John's Worts seem to have shared this reputation—including the one called St. Peter's Wort, *Hypericum tetrapterum*, about which, however, Culpepper delivers one of his most devastating antipapal homilies:

"If Superstition had not been the Father of Tradition, as well as Ignorance the Mother of Devotion, this Herb (as well as *St. John's Wort*) had found some other Name to be known by; but we may say of our Forefathers, as St. *Paul* of the *Athenians*, *I perceive in many Things you are too superstitious*. . . . It riseth up with square upright Stalks for the most Part, some greater and higher than *St. John's Wort* (and good Reason too, St. *Peter* being the greater Apostle, ask the Pope else; for though God would have the Saints equal, the Pope is of another opinion). . . . There is not a Straw to chuse between this and St. *John's Wort*, only St. *Peter* must have it, lest he should want Pot Herbs."

Marshy meadows and stream-sides are especially fascinating in June: Meadow Sweet (also called Queen of the Meadows) is coming out, and the Loosestrife will soon follow; nor can one ignore the Yellow Flag, or English "Flower-de-luce" (it seems a pity we have abandoned this name). And of course the Buttercups—not so much in the water-meadows, but the pastures nearby are golden now with *Ranunculus acris*, the Meadow Crowfoot; and the marshes themselves have buttercups of a kind—for example, *Ranunculus lingua*, the Greater Spearwort, with big flowers an inch and a half across; and *Ranunculus sceleratus*, with its small flowers and curious cylindrical fruits. *Ranunculus sceleratus*, as its name implies, has a bad character: it is, in fact, according to Sowerby, "one of the most virulent of our native plants";

when bruised and applied to the skin, it produces blisters, and the same author tells us that "strolling beggars have been said to use it for that purpose, in order to excite compassion"—a practice which, rather oddly, provoked Sowerby into expressing sentiments which one can only call socialistic: "[it was]," he writes, "a more innocent way of raising money than many practised, on a larger scale, by their superiors, inasmuch as the encouragement of public virtues (however misapplied) is surely better than that of public vices." It is better, in other words, to rub one's skin with the Celery-leaved Crowfoot, than (for instance) to keep a gin-shop or a *bordello*; it seems an odd vindication of *Ranunculus sceleratus*—but one can, I suppose, extract a moral, if one chooses, even from a rather undistinguished (though scelerate) buttercup.

June may be the month of roses, but in northern Europe it is also, pre-eminently, the month of orchids. Why is it, I wonder, that this order has such a peculiar fascination for botanists? Partly, no doubt (at least in Britain), because many native orchids are extremely rare. Yet it is not their rarity alone which makes one prize them so; nor is it entirely their beauty, for some (such as the Twayblade) are distinctly dowdy. It is rather, I think, a quality which all orchids possess, and which one might define, for want of a better word, as "aristocratic"; they have been called the Royal Family of the British flora, and they fully deserve the title. Like human aristocrats, too (and I am referring, here, to England in particular), the orchids tend to be "eccentric": there is something impenetrably queer about the whole order, a quality of strangeness which borders, in some cases, upon the sinister.

The oddity of the orchids can be accounted for, I suppose, though not entirely explained, by their complex and curious methods of growth. Orchids can only exist in a state of symbiosis: their seeds are unable to germinate without the help of certain subterranean fungi; consequently they start life under a grave disadvantage. To compensate for this, the orchid has evolved an extremely elaborate process of reproduction; and the peculiar variations which the orchid flower

exhibits are directed to one end—the effective fertilization of the plant
by the appropriate insect. Orchids, in fact, are more highly organized
for sex than any other order of plants, and illustrate to perfection

> How bend and curl the moist top to the spouse,
> And give and take the vegetable vows;
> How those esteem'd of old but tips and chives,
> Are tender husbands and obedient wives;
> Who live and love within the sacred bower—
> That bridal bed, the vulgar term a flower.[1]

—though one cannot help feeling, so far as the orchids are concerned,
that Crabbe's view of the matter is altogether too conjugal and
respectable.

Many British orchids have a marked predilection for a chalky soil,
and the downs are the best place to look for them—not only on the
open ground, but on bushy slopes among thorn and juniper, and in
the beech-hangers. Commonest of the downland species is *Orchis
maculata*, the Spotted Orchid, which also grows in woods; the downland form is usually the variety *trilobata*. Only less abundant are the
lilac spikes of the Fragrant Orchid, *Gymnadenia conopsea*; the Pyramidal,
Anacamptis pyramidalis, follows it a little later—its conical tufts of bright
crimson are very conspicuous. The extraordinary Bee Orchid is
common enough to be fairly well-known; less familiar is the Fly,
which is of a shyer habit, haunting the shadowy borders of woods and
the chalky banks alongside them. Here, too, one will come on the
White Helleborine, sometimes oddly called the Egg Orchid—its
flowers do (though only faintly) suggest hard-boiled eggs split half-
open to show the yolk; and with it will be growing as often as not
the curious Bird's-nest—a saprophyte, which can easily be passed
over as one of the Broomrapes. The name refers to the root, which
is composed of a tangled mass of tuberous rootlets—not very suggestive
of a bird's nest, but the orchids seem doomed to suffer from unsuitable

[1] Crabbe: *The Parish Register.*

names (the Frog Orchid is nothing like a frog, nor is *Orchis militaris* particularly military; the only authentic case of mimicry is the Bee Orchid, which really is startlingly like its namesake). Gerarde refers to the Bird's-nest as "this bastard and unkindely Satyrion," an uncomplimentary remark which rather loses its force from the fact that the accompanying woodcut shows, not the Bird's-nest Orchid, but a Broomrape.

I cannot mention all the orchids, though I'd like to; forced to be selective, I must single out the two most beautiful—the Greater Butterfly and the Lady. The Butterfly is common in woods and on bushy downlands in June: its elegant white flowers are more like large gnats than butterflies; they are fertilized by moths, and their delicious scent only becomes fully apparent in the evening. The Lady I have mentioned before: its leaves were showing as early as the first of January, but it is seldom in flower till mid-May, and can be seen at its best in early June. I think, myself, it is our most beautiful native wildflower: a reckless statement, but I can at least take refuge in the fact that comparatively few people have ever seen the plant. It is confined to Kent, and was never, one gathers, found much elsewhere, apart from stray colonies in Surrey and one or two odd specimens farther afield. It is pleasant to read that Curtis, writing at the end of the eighteenth century, was familiar with it, and that it grew near enough to London to be included in the *Flora Londiniensis*. "On chalky banks," he writes, "abounding with Milkwort and Juniper, near woods and in the woods themselves, in many parts of Kent, especially about Rochester, we have had no small pleasure in observing this plant grow in great abundance." It may be added that the present writer has no small pleasure in confirming Curtis's words, which still, happily, apply to-day. A. D. Webster, writing in the eighteen-nineties,[1] lamented that the Lady Orchid was "becoming fast extinct in the few places where it was known to exist," but fortunately Webster was misinformed, for the Lady is, if anything, on the increase, and is still abundant, as it was in Anne Pratt's day, "in the woodlands and on the

[1] A. D. Webster, *British Orchids*, 2nd edition, 1898.

bushy hill." Miss Pratt records that it was often "carried into the towns in baskets for sale," and it still is—or was until recently.

Even for the least botanically-minded the Lady is an exciting plant to find: its large, compact spikes tower above the dowdy thickets of dog's-mercury with a regal splendour. The upper part of the flower is striped and stippled with deep brownish-purple, contrasting sharply with the pale pink or almost white "lip," which has the air of a butterfly emerging from its chrysalis. According to the books, a Kentish name for the Lady is "Maids of Kent"; I regret to say, however, that I have never heard this used myself. Country people in the districts where it grows usually call it the "Brown Orchid" or "Old Ladies"; though I have also heard it called the "Military Orchid"—a misnomer which has sometimes made my heart miss a beat, but one can be pretty sure that, if one is told where to find "Military Orchids" in Kent, they will always turn out to be Ladies.

By the end of June, the "high midsummer pomps" are in full swing, and the best of the year (to my mind) is over: the young leaves are already fading into the rusty, blackish-green of late summer, the hay is cut, and the corn on the turn. The longest day is past; the year pauses, like a woman *sur le retour*, glancing backward nostalgically towards the "primal burst of bloom"; the last bluebells wither in the copses; the hedges put out their tawdry July finery—Knapweed, Scabious, Agrimony—but the best is over, and the evenings fall with a sense of fulfilment: soon we shall be saying "The days are drawing in"; but in this brief moment of equilibrium before the deluge, the twilight lingers, timelessly, still cool with the coolness of early summer, and fragrant with the early roses—

> Roses that down the alleys shine afar,
> And open, jasmine-muffled lattices,
> And groups under the dreaming garden-trees,
> And the full moon and the white evening star.[1]

[1] Matthew Arnold, *Thyrsis*.

July

La maison serait pleine de roses et de guêpes.
On y entendrait, l'après-midi, sonner les vêpres;
et les raisins couleur de pierre transparente
sembleraient dormir au soleil sous l'ombre lente.

THESE lines of Francis Jammes have strayed into these pages, I'm afraid, for no better reason than because I happen to like them; however, I at least have the excuse that Jammes is not much read in this country—nor are his works readily accessible. Moreover, he is preeminently the poet of high summer: his poems are laden with the heavy, languorous airs of hot afternoons in country gardens and in houses "full of roses and wasps"—houses of some remote and æstival cloud-cuckoo-land, haunted by the cool ghosts of little girls from Victorian magazines, with names like Clara d'Ellébeuse. . . .

July—the word itself has an opulent, golden warmth, the second syllable broadens into a positive blaze of yellow sunlight. It is the month of dog-days—our grandfathers (and even our fathers) hated it: the characters in Victorian novels frequently succumbed, during July, to those mysterious diseases—"low" or "putrid" fevers, "decline," greensickness—which seem to have been so prevalent during the nineteenth century. In one of the less-known novels of Wilkie Collins—I forget which—the action comes to a gory climax in July, which is referred to, in the previous chapters, as the "dreaded month": not, as one had supposed, because some "bill" was to be honoured, or some murderous pact fulfilled, but merely because of the hot weather—which could be depended upon to kill off all but the lustiest and youngest of the characters.

Why did we suddenly—some twenty or thirty years ago—cease thus to be "allergic" to heat, and (flying to the other extreme) become sun-worshippers? The sun-bathing cult would have seemed stark insanity to the Victorians—or even, for that matter, to the Edwardians; they would as soon have bared their bodies to the snows of January. To explain this odd phenomenon by saying, merely, that our ideas of "hygiene" have changed, that we wear less clothes, etc., seems to me inadequate; we sunbathe only incidentally for health reasons: mostly, we do it because we like it. The mystery, so far as I can see, remains insoluble.

We visited the downs last month in search of orchids; now, in July, most of these are going over—except the Pyramidal, and perhaps a belated Bee. But other downland flowers are in their full glory: Rock Rose, Yellow-wort, Centaury and the Clustered Bellflower. Centaury belongs to the gentian family, so does Yellow-wort, though they are not much alike; both contain the bitter principle used in tonics and apéritifs. Centaury in particular was valued by the herbalists as a "stomachic," and, a generation ago, was still, to my knowledge, used for this purpose in East Kent: but it is used no longer. I mentioned "greensickness" just now, and it may be noted that Culpepper strongly recommends Centaury for this singular complaint; it was, he says, "much used by the *Italians* in Powder for that Purpose," though one would have supposed that greensickness was a nordic rather than a meridional disease. " 'Tis very wholesome," adds Culpepper, "but not very toothsome."

More flamboyant than these "gentians" is the Viper's Bugloss, that most magnificent (English) member of the Borage family. Its tall blue spikes, when seen in the mass, have an extraordinary intensity of hue, seeming almost to sizzle in the hot downland air. The name is said to be derived from a fancied resemblance of the seeds to a viper's head—hence, by the doctrine of signatures, the plant was held to be a specific against snake-bite. The flowers are particularly attractive to bees who, as the author of *Wild Flowers Worth Notice* observes, are greedy in their "depredations." "But we must not," adds Mrs. Lankester hastily, unwilling to let slip the chance of drawing a moral, "we must not consider these little creatures as merely selfish seekers of their own gratification; they, in common with the whole of creation, serve great purposes, and carry out the designs of the Great Architect of all. . . ."

Another member of the Borage family found on the downs is the Hound's-tongue—a dull-looking plant with bluish-purple flowers, reputed (according to Gerarde) to cure "the disease called *Ignis sacer*, or wilde fire." Was this hydrophobia? It seems probable, for Hound's-tongue (*Cynoglossum*), according to Culpepper, was effective against the bites of mad dogs, whence it appears to have derived its name—a curious reversal of the commoner process by which the curative properties of a plant were deduced from its particular "signature." In the case of Hound's-tongue, this appears to be absent—unless the leaves are supposed to resemble the tongue of a dog, which seems far-fetched. "These leaves," Gerarde observes, "stinke very filthily, much like unto the pisse of dogs: wherefore the Dutch men have called it Hound's pisse, and not Hound's-toong." Culpepper quotes Mizaldus as saying that "the leaves laid under the Feet, will keep the Dogs from barking at you"—presumably for the olfactory reason referred to by Gerarde. This property, according to Culpepper, accounts for the name—"Hound's-tongue, because it ties the Tongues of Hounds, whether it be true or not, I never tried; yet I cured the biting of a mad Dog with this only Medicine."

Nobody, I suppose, is much attached to thistles; yet some are attractive enough—the Musk Thistle, for instance, with its big, drooping flowers, often abundant on the downs; and even the Dwarf Thistle, with almost stalkless flowers springing straight from the turf, has its points—in more senses than one; anybody who has sat down rather too suddenly on the downs in summer will be fundamentally familiar with it. More distinguished (and more rare) is Our Lady's Thistle, also known as the Milk Thistle, with drooping mauve flowers and large, very prickly leaves curiously veined with milky white: a monkish legend relates that the Christ-child, having removed his lips from the breast, allowed the spilt milk to fall upon this plant—hence its popular names.

Such Marian derivations of plant-names are innumerable: indeed, there is almost no attribute of the Mother of God which is not thus honoured—her slippers, smock, bed-straw, fingers, mantle and many more are duly commemorated in the British flora, and the practice is by no means confined to Britain. Brand, in his *Popular Antiquities*, quotes from a curious work, *The Welsh Levite tossed in a Blanket*: "I remember the blessed times, when every thing in the World that was displeasing and offensive to the Brethren went under the name of horrid Abominable Popish Superstition. Organs and May Poles, Bishops' Courts and the Bear Garden, Surplices and long Hair, Cathedrals and Play Houses, Set Forms and Painted Glass, Fonts and Apostle Spoons. . . . Nay, in our zeal we visited the Gardens and Apothecary's shops. *Unguentum Apostolicum*, *Carduus benedictus*, *Angelica*, *St. John's Wort*, and *Our Lady's Thistle*, were summoned before a Class, and commanded to take new Names."

Another thistle whose name commemorates a legend (though not a Marian one this time) is *Carlina vulgaris*, the Carline Thistle, which is said to have been the plant employed by Charlemagne, under divine guidance, as a cure for the pestilence which ravaged his armies. This, however, seems to have been the only occasion on which the Carline Thistle exhibited any curative properties: Gerarde dismisses it as being "of no use," and the other herbalists seem also to have ignored it.

I have spoken before of the ecological "associations" of wild plants— the woodland flora, for instance, typically composed of bluebells, campion, wood spurge and so on; but many of these floral groupings are even more sharply defined and exclusive—for example, the flora of mountain and moorland bogs on a peaty, acid soil. Sundew, Butterwort, Bog Asphodel, Cotton-grass—the bog plants are marked by a characteristic oddity which, like that of the orchids, is doubtless

conditioned by their unusual modes of growth. Like the orchids, too—
and with more reason, perhaps—they have acquired a rather sinister
reputation: Sundew and Butterwort are both carnivorous, and the
Asphodel (which has no connection, by the way, with the classical
plant), though in fact harmless enough, was believed to rot the
bones of cattle which cropped it—a legend which is commemorated
in its Latin specific name, *ossifragum*. There are three species of Sundew,
of which by far the commonest is the Round-leaved, *Drosera rotundifolia*: its glandular leaf-hairs secrete a sticky fluid, to which small insects
adhere; thus trapped, they are subsequently assimilated and digested
by the plant. The drops of sticky moisture were formerly believed to
be dew, which the plant appeared to have the mysterious property of
retaining, even in the hottest sunshine: hence the name. It was known
also as *Rosa Solis*; oddly enough, the older botanical writers seem to
have been unaware of its insectivorous properties. "Cattle of the
female kinde," says Gerarde, "are stirred up to lust by eating even of a
small quantitie," but the Sundew seems to have been of little value in
herbal medicine—though Burton quotes Bernardus Perrottus as
"[preferring] his *herba solis* before all the rest" in the treatment of
melancholy; and Culpepper recommends it for "Qualms and Passions
of the Heart."

Butterwort is less obviously an insectivore than Sundew: its leaves
are without hairs, but secrete an oily juice, sufficiently adherent to
capture small insects, which are in due course absorbed and digested.
The rosette of smooth, rather liliaceous-looking leaves seem to belong
to some monocotyledonous plant, and the spurred, purple flower
has an incongruous air, suggesting that the Butterwort is trying to
pass itself off as a mere harmless violet. Like most of the other bog
plants, it was supposed to be harmful to cattle: the plain fact being
that boggy ground makes poor pasture, whatever the quality of the
vegetation; one would hardly expect cattle to thrive on it, but farmers
nowadays no longer blame the Butterwort.

"The plant is called by the Laplanders *Tätgrass*," says Miss Pratt,
"and the leaves are used by them in preparing a favourite beverage of

milk, which they call *Taeotmioelk*. The fresh leaves of the Butterwort are laid upon a filter, and warm reindeer's milk is poured upon them, which . . . is allowed to remain for one or two days, till [it] becomes sour." Gerarde refers to the plant as "Yorkshire Sanicle," and tells us that "The husbandmen's wives of Yorkshire, do use to annoint the dugs of their kine with the fat and oilous juice of the herbe Butterwoort, when they are bitten with any venemous worm, or chapped, rifted, and hurt by any other meanes."

Bog Asphodel is more conspicuous than the Butterworts and the Sundews, but hardly so impressive as its name might lead one to expect. Its sedge-like leaves and small yellow flowers suggest something between a rush and a lily, and in fact the Asphodel is a border-line case, formerly included in the Rush family, but now considered to be a true lily: it has at least, one would imagine, a better claim (judged merely by appearances) than certain other unlikely members of the order, such as Herb Paris and Butcher's Broom.

The Asphodel is a pretty enough plant, but attains to its full splendour only when the flowers are over, and the seed-vessels are ripening; the whole spike is then tinged with a deep orange-crimson, suggesting at a distance some unusually coloured orchid. . . . Another bog plant worth a glance is the Buck-bean or Bog-bean—a member of the gentian family, with spikes of curious pinkish-white flowers which have the air of some elaborate confectionery: the petals are covered with white, hair-like filaments, and suggest the sugary fantastications which decorate a wedding-cake. Buck-bean is rather a local plant nowadays, though abundant enough in some districts; it cannot, alas, be found now as it could in Curtis's day in "*Battersea Meadows*, particularly about a hundred yards distant from the *Red House* towards *Chelsea*. . . ."[1]

In the water-meadows and riverside marshes a host of rank, luxuriant plants jostle for position—Willowherb, Meadow Sweet, Loosestrife purple and yellow, Hemp Agrimony: from this lush jungle I shall be content to pick out two rarities for special mention this month. One is the Marsh Sow-thistle, *Sonchus palustris*—a plant so

[1] *Flora Londiniensis.*

rare nowadays that few botanists can ever have seen it growing. Everybody knows the Common Sow-thistle, most squalid and persistent of garden weeds; almost as common is the Corn Sow-thistle, with its big, dandelion-like flowers. *Sonchus palustris* is similar to the last, but it is the giant of the genus, attaining a height of nine or ten feet: the flowers, however, are comparatively small and insignificant. In Curtis's day it was to be found "sparingly in the marshes about Blackwall and Poplar"; half a century later it was nearly extinct: "I am not aware" (says Sowerby) "that it is to be found now [1865] except among beds of reeds . . . behind Plumstead Butts, immediately below Woolwich." Curiously enough, the recorded localities for the Sow-thistle have never been very far from the metropolis: it survives, to this day, in a marsh near Snodland, among the squalid surroundings of a cement-works, and appears to flourish. As a "composite" plant, capable of producing a quantity of wind-borne seed, its rarity is hard to account for.

My other riverside rarity is the Monkshood, *Aconitum napellus:* this is the true Aconite, not to be confused with the yellow Winter Aconite, which it doesn't in the least resemble, though both belong to the Buttercup family. Most people are familiar with Monkshood as a garden flower: it is not unlike a delphinium, but with duller purple, hooded flowers and more finely-divided foliage. In the wild state it appears to be confined to a few stream-sides in the counties bordering on the Bristol Channel (this district has several "specialities," including the Bristol Rock-cress and the Wasp Orchid, *Ophrys Trollii*). I have only once, myself, seen the Monkshood growing wild: I say "seen" rather than "found," for my view of it was from a train, travelling along the Glamorgan coast; unfortunately the spot was too far from my destination to be revisited on foot. . . . Sir J. E. Smith, in his *English Flora* (1829) records it from Herefordshire, "by the side of the river Teme . . . to all appearance truly wild." The same author gives another locality: "In watery ground on both sides of a brook, at Ford, near Wiveliscomb, Somersetshire, in great plenty, for the course of a mile or more." It is an odd fact that the Monkshood (like the Marsh Sow-thistle) though very rare and local, is extremely abundant in the few places where it occurs.

Henry Phillips, in his *Flora Historica*, quotes from a French poem whose author he does not mention:

> L'Aconit, au sac malfaisant,
> Comme s'il s'armait pour la guerre
> Elève un casque ménaçant . . .

Monkshood, in fact, is one of a number of poisonous plants which really *look* poisonous: its "casque ménaçant" has a curiously lurid tinge of purple, and the suggestion of a monk's cowl, commemorated by the popular name, adds to the sinister impression. Monkshood has, in fact, a Black Record—blacker even than that of the Deadly Nightshade. It is probably the most venomous plant in the British Flora, though one cannot help wondering at the carelessness of those who have died, as Anne Pratt records, "by mistaking the root for horseradish." Nothing could be more unlike horseradish than the finely-divided leaf of the Monkshood; yet the number of deaths from aconite poisoning by far outnumber those caused by any other plant. "Some persons," says Maund, in his *Botanic Garden*, "discard all species of it from the garden," though he adds that "this would, to most florists, appear rather fastidious, inasmuch as the English are not so passionately attached to vegetable diet, as to eat garden herbage indiscriminately." None the less, if you are unfortunate enough to have eaten Monkshood root shredded with your Sunday beef, all you have to do, according to an unnamed "Greek physician" quoted by Maund, is to boil "the plant Eryngion . . . in the broth of a goose," which was apparently considered an infallible antidote. Should this fail (or the ingredients be unobtainable at short notice) "the broth of an old cock" may be tried as an alternative.

The alkaloid principle of aconite acts rapidly upon the central nervous system, producing delirium and convulsions. It is said that Monkshood was one of the ingredients in the "flying" ointment employed by witches; and a theory has been advanced that aconite, applied thus by inunction, may have produced a hallucinatory state in which the patient believed himself to be flying through the air. It is even possible that the many extant accounts of the Sabbath itself may owe something to the visions induced by aconite.[1]

The waysides and hedgerows have, by mid-July, taken on a rather overblown and tawdry air: the more delicate plants of June have been elbowed aside by the coarser growths of late summer—Knapweed, Scabious, Agrimony, innumerable thistles, and the ubiquitous Umbellifers. In chalky districts, the large Knapweed, or Hard-heads (*Centaurea scabiosa*) is common: its big, flaunting, purple flowers are attractive enough, but the plant is of a tough, sinewy growth, and, if gathered and arranged with other flowers in a vase, has an awkward and clodhopperish air, like some handsome peasant who has been invited into an upper-class drawing-room. The same is true of the Succory (or Wild Chicory), whose exquisite sky-blue flowers are borne on obstinately unmanageable stems. Nor is Agrimony very pleasing, once removed from the hedgeside: and nobody nowadays, I suppose, gathers it as a cure for the itch, though, according to Woodville,[2] it "manifests great efficacy" in the treatment of that unpleasant complaint. The big Field Scabious, which we used to call "Pincushions" when I was a child, is at its best in cornfields; by the wayside, it is apt to collect a film of dust and to appear rather raffish and untidy. "These flowers," says Sowerby,[3] "held over the smoke of a pipe of tobacco, in a few minutes become of a most beautiful green, from the alkaline nature of the smoke, to which their delicate purple is peculiarly sensible." They could, in fact, be used instead of red litmus-paper; and one wonders if they were, perhaps, employed in the nineties as a substitute (among the poor but epicene) for the green carnation.

Rest-harrow is not the most attractive of the Pea family—its angular

---

[1] See Margaret Murray: *The Witch Cult in Western Europe;* also E. M. Butler: *Ritual Magic,* etc.

[2] *Medical Botany.*

[3] *English Botany* (1799).

stems sprawl untidily, and the dull pink flowers lack the charm of some of the other vetches; yet I have always had a fondness for it, and once, many years ago, even tried to read the novel by Maurice Hewlett which is named after it—an attempt which was, I regret to say, unsuccessful. According to Parkinson, a decoction of Rest-harrow "made with some vinegar and gargled in the mouth easeth the pains of the toothache, especially when it cometh of rheum." The same author records that "in former times . . . the young shoots and tender stalks were pickled up to be eaten as a meate or sause, wonderfully commended against a foul breath, and to take away the smell of wine in them that had drunke too much."

I have spoken before of Betony, a tall, crimson-flowered plant of the Mint family, common in woods and hedgerows. Its reputation as a magical and medicinal herb was once second to none; yet nowadays, so far as I know, it has no "virtues" whatever. Less potent, but of considerable use in magic and ritual, were the Mulleins: commonest of the group is *Verbascum thapsus*, the Great Mullein, which may have been the species used in a ceremony recorded by Frazer:

"Bonfires were lit in almost all the hamlets of Poitou on the Eve of St. John. People marched round them thrice, carrying a branch of walnut in their hand. Shepherdesses and children passed sprigs of mullein (*verbascum*) and nuts across the flames; the nuts were supposed to cure toothache, and the mullein to protect the cattle from sickness and sorcery."[1]

An old name for Mullein was "Hig-taper," and I have heard the name Aaron's Rod attached to it, though this properly belongs to another plant. Many of the older plant names seem inexplicable: why "Toadflax," for instance? The leaves of the Yellow Toadflax (abundant now on roadsides and field-borders) are somewhat like those of flax; one can only assume that the prefix "toad" is a mere ill-defined term of denigration, like the similar "dog" and "horse" (e.g., Dog's Mercury, Horse Chestnut). Yellow Toadflax is a charming plant however, despite its name: it is a truly wild Snapdragon—the

[1] *Golden Bough* (abr. edition), p. 629.

garden "Antirrhinum" occurs here and there in a wild state, but is not a true native; nor is the Ivy-leaved Toadflax, which covers old walls with its round leaves and tiny purple flowers: it has been established, however, for several centuries, and Parkinson records that it grew "naturally in divers places of our land."

The practice of "naturalizing" foreign plants in Britain is frowned upon by botanists, whose carefully kept records are liable to be confused by these immigrants; such strictures, however, seem to me the height of pedantry: many plants now considered truly indigenous were imported by our forefathers, and I see no reason for excluding newcomers to-day. A hundred years ago, botanists seem to have been less xenophobic: "We would be content," says Maund, in his *Botanic Garden*, "to register Britain's legitimate post-diluvian Flora as it now stands . . . and encourage all to become disseminators of new beauties over our native land, for the benefit and gratification of future generations." I am inclined, myself, to agree; but to most botanists such sentiments would seem the rankest heresy.

I have spoken already of the rôle of the blitz in disseminating such local plants as the Oxford Ragwort and the Rose-bay Willowherb. To these may be added two of our native "lettuces," *Lactuca virosa* and *Lactuca serriola*; both of these were rare before the war, but have since become comparatively common in the Home Counties, particularly *Lactuca virosa*, which covers the blitzed sites at Canterbury and elsewhere. This plant is said to be the original of our garden lettuces, but the relationship is hard to credit: *Lactuca virosa* is a coarse-leaved plant with a fœtid odour, and even the young shoots (which I have tried) are intolerably bitter.

Two other plants likely to be found in the blitzed areas are Clary and the yellow Stone-crop. The latter is a familiar ornament of old walls and the roofs of cottages: it is the commonest of our native stone-crops, and was known in former days as Prick-Madam—a name whose derivation may be left, as Sowerby said of the Fumitory, to "those more sapient than ourselves." According to Woodville,[1] the

[1] *Medical Botany*.

Stone-crop "acts powerfully on the primae viae," and is both emetic and cathartic; it was administered in the form of a decoction in beer, but, adds Woodville rather depressingly, "milk has been found to answer this purpose better than beer. . . ." Clary, another haunter of old walls and dry hedge-banks, was once believed to be efficacious in diseases of the eye—hence, presumably, the name. To Gerarde it was known as *Oculus Christi*: "the seede put whole into the eies" (he says) "clenseth and purgeth them exceedingly from waterish humours, rednesse, inflammation, and divers other maladies." "In some parts of the country," says Sowerby, "Clary flowers are made into a wine," which, he adds (with a suspicious lack of enthusiasm), "is liked by the people of the district."

I have already spoken of the Nightshades, deadly and otherwise, but without referring to the most romantically-named of the lot— Enchanter's Nightshade, *Circea lutetiana*. Why this plant was ever so christened remains a mystery; not only is it not a Nightshade at all (it belongs, in fact, to the Willowherb family), but it has, apparently, no magical—or even medicinal—virtues whatever. It has been suggested (rather feebly) that the name is derived from its habit of frequenting shady, gloomy places where Circean enchantments are likely to prevail; as it happens, however, *Circea* is quite as much at home in suburban gardens as in any "ghoul-haunted woodland." Nor is its appearance in the least sinister: a drab little plant, with small, wax-pink flowers. According to Gerarde, it seems to have been con-fused, at one time, with the Mandrake—though there is not the faintest resemblance between the two. "There is no use of this herbe," Gerarde writes, "either in Phisicke or Chirurgerie that I can read of, which hath happened by the corruption of time, and the errour of some who have taken Mandragoras for Circea, in which errour they have still persisted unto this daie." Sowerby, however, has another theory to account for the plant's "romantic name," and quotes certain "old writers" (unnamed) who "tell us its principal use is for amorous purposes; but how it is to be applied they are silent."

August

The shutter of time darkening ceaselessly
Has whisked away the foam of may and elder
And I realize how now, as every year before,
Once again the gay months have eluded me . . .

While the lawn-mower sings moving up and down
Spirting its little fountain of vivid green,
I, like Poussin, make a still-bound fête of us
Suspending every noise, of insect or machine . . .[1]

"A STILL-BOUND FÊTE"—August has its own equilibrium, opposed to
that of January; they are the positive and negative poles of the year.
August, the classical month, a fête by Poussin in which "Time is shown
with a stone face" against the heavy, rusty-black masses of the trees;
yet Time is not static, the calm, Augustan days are pregnant with the
seed of their own destruction, there is a sense, in the balanced quietude,
of *après moi le déluge*.

For the botanist, if the "gay months" have eluded him, August
provides a kind of delayed *deuxième service*—the July flowers lingering
on, but with few new arrivals to distract his calm appraisal. I can think
of less than half a dozen plants which positively bloom for the first
time in August, and even they belong, more properly, to September—
Meadow Saffron and the Lady's Tresses Orchid, for instance, are really
"autumn" flowers. Another orchid, the Broad-leaved Helleborine, is
I suppose a true flower of August, though it may be out by the end
of July: a handsome plant whose broad and very orchidaceous-looking
leaves seem to promise some spectacular and exotic bloom; but the

[1] Louis MacNeice: *August*.

123

flowers are rather small and dingy, and unworthy of the *ensemble*. More attractive is the rarer Violet Helleborine, *Epipactis violacea*, a saprophytic plant tinged from top to toe with dull purple; there are yet other Helleborines, rarer still, but, like the Marsh Orchids, they are a confused and confusing group, and not very rewarding to anybody but the specialist.

August for the people and their favourite islands . . .[1]

—and the seaside is no bad place to botanize this month. The maritime flora is fascinating—where it has been allowed to survive undisturbed; the "development" of coastal resorts has, however, wrought havoc in too many cases, and our seaside flora is not what it was. I believe the Starry Clover still survives on a single patch of foreshore at Shoreham; I hope so, anyway—but probably its days are numbered. In my childhood I remember Camber Sands, near Rye, as an unrivalled community of maritime plants; but a large holiday-camp has since reduced it to a mere sandy desert. Yet the sea flora is, fortunately, fairly persistent, and one can still botanize with some satisfaction on the

> Outskirts of the Borough reach . . .
> Where hang at open doors the net and cork,
> While squalid sea-dames mend the meshy work . . .[2]

and by the edge of the salt marshes where

> Samphire banks and saltwort bound the flood

—a reference which, by the way, Crabbe is careful to explain in a footnote: "The jointed glasswort, *Salicornia*, is here meant, not the true Samphire, the *Crithmum maritimum*."

> There, fed by food they love, to rankest size,
> Around the dwellings docks and wormwood rise;
> Here the strong mallow strikes her slimy root,
> Here the dull nightshade hangs her deadly fruit:

[1] W. H. Auden: *Look, Stranger!*
[2] Crabbe: *The Borough.*

124

On hills of dust the henbane's faded green,
And pencill'd flower of sickly scent is seen;
At the wall's base the fiery nettle springs,
With fruit globose and fierce with poison'd stings;
Above (the growth of many a year) is spread
The yellow level of the Stone-crop's bed . . .
These, with our sea-weeds, rolling up and down,
Form the contracted Flora of the town.[1]

Oddly enough, Crabbe fails to mention either here or, I think, elsewhere, the two most handsome and curious plants of the seaside's "contracted Flora"—Horned Poppy and Sea Holly. This is the more odd as the Poppy (if not the Sea Holly) is still common at Aldeburgh, and must have been there in Crabbe's day. It is an entirely charming plant, and less well-known than it deserves to be; the large, golden-yellow flowers seem curiously delicate by contrast with the tough, wiry stems upon which they are borne, and the long, curving "horns" add a touch of almost surrealist fantasy to the plant when the flowers have faded. Anne Pratt includes it in her small book on poisonous plants, and remarks elsewhere that the root "is said, if eaten, to occasion madness"—but one can hardly imagine anybody mistaking the Horned Poppy for any edible plant.

The roots of Sea Holly, on the other hand, are (or perhaps one should say were) edible: we have Shakespeare's word for it, among others—the "eringoes," mentioned in *The Merry Wives* (and perhaps elsewhere) were none other than Sea Holly roots. Gerarde provides the following recipe for "conditing" them:

"Refine sugar fit for the purpose, and take a pound of it, the white of one egge, and a pint of cleere water, boile them togither and scum it, then let it boile untill it be come to a good strong syruppe, and when it is boiled, as it cooleth adde thereto a sawcer full of Rose water, a spoonful of Cinnamon water, and a graine of Muske, which have beene infused togither the night before, and now strained." The boiled roots were infused in this mixture, and then baked: "In this manner

[1] Crabbe: *The Borough.*

if you condite your rootes, there is not any that can prescribe you a better way. And thus may you condite any other roote whatsoever, which will not onely be exceeding delicate, but very wholesome. . . ."

The use of "eringoes," as an alternative to olives and salted almonds at cocktail-parties, seems hardly likely to be revived; nor, for that matter, is the Sea Holly as common as it was formerly—it is one of the plants which have been diminished by the activities of Mr. Butlin and his colleagues; yet it is still fairly abundant on some parts of the coast. Its singular and haunting beauty has appealed to painters—particularly to the late Paul Nash, in whose earlier pictures the Sea Holly occurs more than once.

The Sea Convolvulus is another pleasant seaside plant neglected by Crabbe: its small fleshy leaves and large pink flowers trail over the sand-dunes among the clumps of marram. Nearby, in the damp fringes of the salt-marsh, and in the marshes themselves, one will come upon the Sea Aster, that fleshy-leaved, wild "Michaelmas Daisy" which has always the air of having escaped from some neighbouring garden; yet it is a truly wild plant. So is the Gladdon or Roast-beef Plant, though it has a tendency to frequent cliff-side gardens and plantations. Perhaps it shouldn't be counted as a seaside flower; it can occur farther inland, but seems to thrive best within sight and sound of the sea. It is a rather dull-looking little iris—not to be compared with the handsome Yellow Flag of the inland marshes; it is, however, one of those plants which compensate for their insignificant flowers by the splendour of their fruits: the Gladdon produces tight clusters of scarlet berries which persist well into the winter, and may sometimes still be found in the following spring.

The name "Roast-beef Plant" is a matter for some dispute: "The leaves," says Sowerby,[1] "when bruised, have a very peculiar offensive smell, which gave occasion to the trivial name; yet this smell having some resemblance to the effluvia of roast beef, the name of Roast-beef Plant has been as a title of honour to this Iris." Many people, including myself, would agree that the Gladdon deserves its "title of honour"—

[1] *English Botany* (1799).

the odour does seem to me to suggest that of rather "high" meat; to others, however, it would appear to be aptly described by the plant's Latin specific name—*fœtidissima*.

> BOTANIC MUSE! who in this latter age
> Led by your airy hand the Swedish sage,
> Bad his keen eye your secret haunts explore
> On dewy dell, high wood and winding shore;
> Say on each leaf how tiny Graces dwell;
> How laugh the pleasures in a blossom's bell;
> How insect Loves arise on cobweb wings,
> Aim their light shafts, and point their little stings . . .[1]

But the Botanic Muse, though she may have led Linnæus by her "airy hand," has proved, I think, a rather coy mistress to most poets, disposing her favours in unlikely places, and never for long at a time. Arnold and Hopkins (as I have remarked already) seem to have been especially favoured; but poetic references to flowers have, on the whole, a distressing tendency to be either intolerably arch and winsome, or downright inaccurate. It is the same with fiction: novelists will persist in referring to Beaked Parsley (for instance) as "Fennel" or "Hemlock"; their bluebells flower in August, their roses in April. Poets, on the whole, tend to be more accurate than novelists: yet even Arnold could call the Field Convolvulus "blue," and refer to "red" Loosestrife when he meant "purple."

The Loosestrife is, surely, indisputably purple—it has even been portrayed (mistakenly) by Millais as the "long purples" of Ophelia's garland. In my childhood, it had a special fascination for me, chiefly because, for many years, I never managed to find it; there were few marshes round my home, and it wasn't till my family went to stay at Camberley that I did, at last, find the Loosestrife. . . . On the same occasion, too, I found Heather for the first time—not only the Common Heather and the Ling, but the Cross-leaved Heath, *Erica*

[1] Erasmus Darwin: *The Loves of the Plants.*

tetralix, which I thought then and still think the most attractive of the commoner species. Its small, pale-pink clusters are never so abundant as the Common Heath and Ling among which it grows, and are apt to be overlooked. Such, it seems, has always been the case: "it is wonderful," writes Sir J. E. Smith,[1] "that this most elegant, and not uncommon, plant is scarcely delineated at all by the old authors; nor by any of them correctly."

The Heath family is an odd one, including as it does a number of plants which one would never suspect of belonging to it at all—the saprophytic Fir-rape, for instance, which looks more like a Broom-rape or an orchid than a near relation of the heather; equally incongruous seem the Winter-greens and the Strawberry Tree. The Gentians, too, are a varied tribe: Yellow-wort or Buck-bean seem far removed from most people's idea of a gentian. The Felwort, however—*Gentiana amarella*—is recognizably related to its alpine cousins; though it is something of a poor relation, with its stubby growth and its clusters of dull purple flowers. It is common on chalk-downs and dry pastures this month, and lingers on, with a number of other downland plants, well into September. With it, as often as not, one will find the Eyebright, an inconspicuous little flower which, like the Clary, had a great reputation for improving the eyesight. "If this Herb," says Culpepper, "were but as much used as it is neglected, it would half spoil the Spectaclemakers' Trade; and a Man would think, that Reason should teach People to prefer the Preservation of their natural before artificial spectacles."

It seems possible that Eyebright may really have been of some use in conjunctivitis and such complaints; but the medicinal claims of the Devil's-bit Scabious are founded on pure sympathetic magic. I have referred before to the curious and persistent legends about this plant, which survived well into the nineteenth century, and can be traced back at least as far as William Turner, the "Father of British Botany," who writes that "some use to geve the pouder" (of Devil's-bit) "into the bodye to kill wormes, and to lay the herbe onto bruised places, or bitten

[1] Sir J. E. Smith: *The English Flora*, Vol. II (1828).

places, or to such places that be bruised by fallinge." Legends quite apart, the Devil's-bit is a pretty enough plant, with its purple, button-like heads; it is equally at home on open pastures or in the woods.

A more familiar woodland plant of late summer is perhaps the Teazel, whose prickly heads, stained with gold or crimson, are some-times sold in the London streets: the Teazel, however (like the Lily), is scarcely improved by being gilded, and is quite decorative enough in its natural state. It was once used as a kind of poor man's weather-glass: "being gathered and hanged up in the House where the air may come freely to it, upon the alteration of cold and windy weather, [the head] will grow smoother, and against Rain will close up his prickles."[1]

Less common than the Teazel, though frequent in some woodland districts, is the Orpine: the most handsome British member of the Stone-crop family. Its flattened heads of pink flowers are often seen in gardens, but it is a truly wild plant, and was one of the herbs myster-iously associated with the ceremonies of Midsummer Eve. Its popular name was Midsummer Men, and as lately as the eighteenth century, it seems, a country girl "would never go to bed on Midsummer Eve, without sticking up in her room the well-known plant called Mid-summer Men, as the bending of the leaves to the right, or to the left, would never fail to tell her whether her lover was true or false."[2]

Little can be said in favour of the Common Ragwort, whose dusty, untidy yellow corymbs cover every waste patch at this time of year. Its raggedness is often partly due, as a matter of fact, to the ravages of the Cinnabar Caterpillar, which feeds upon it; it is, however, a squalid, unpleasant plant, and the Oxford Ragwort (which I've mentioned before) is to be preferred to it. Why the Oxford species should be called *Senecio squalidus* I have never been able to discover: it is less inelegant than most of its British relations (among which is the Groundsel), though since the blitz one sees rather too much of it.

[1] Willsford: *Nature's Secrets*, quoted by Brand (*Popular Antiquities*).
[2] *Tawney Rachel, or the Fortune-Teller*, quoted by Brand.

The Ragworts, if somewhat plebeian in themselves, are well-connected, being closely related to those magnificent purple and crimson Cinerarias which deck the "lounges" of expensive hotels.

The roadsides and hedge-banks in August are ablaze, still, with the flowers of July, overgrown now, and coated, as often as not, with a thick film of dust. An ugly but not uninteresting roadside plant is the Mugwort; its crushed leaves have the unmistakable odour of absinthe, which is in fact made from an allied species, *Artemisia absinthium*. Mugwort itself is one of several plants to which a curious superstition attached itself: "It is certainly and constantly affirmed" (runs one plausible account) "that on Midsummer Eve there is found, under the root of Mugwort, a coal which saves or keeps them safe from the plague, carbuncle, lightning, the Quartan ague, and from burning, that bear the same about them: and Mizaldus, the writer hereof, saith, that he doth hear that it is to be found the same day under the root of plantain, which I know to be of truth, for *I have found them* the same day under the root of plantain, which is especially and chiefly to be found at noon."[1]

Aubrey, in his *Miscellanies*, has a variant of this story: "On the day of St. John Baptist (1694) I accidentally was walking in the pasture behind Montague House, it was twelve o'clock, I saw there about two or three and twenty young women, most of them well habited, on their knees, very busie, as if they had been weeding. A young man told me that they were looking for a coal under the root of a plantain, to put under their heads that night, and they should dream who would be their husbands."

On hedge-banks and roadsides in late summer one sometimes comes across a tall, handsome plant with clusters of pink flowers which— since it is uncommon, and often occurs near villages—seems to have escaped from a garden. This is the Soapwort, *Saponaria officinalis*: it is, in fact, a "doubtful native," but appears to have been well-established

[1] Lupton: *Notable Things*, quoted by Brand (italics Brand's).

by Gerarde's time, for he speaks of it as growing "wilde of it selfe neere to rivers and running brookes in sunnie places," besides being "planted in gardens for the flowers sake, to the decking up of houses." It has "no use in phisicke," according to Gerarde, but Curtis[1] tells us that "it has been recommended in venereal and scrophulous diseases." The plant produces a mucilaginous juice which, says Gerarde, "scowreth almost as well as Sope"—hence the name.

Marjoram is another pleasant wayside plant, whose evocative name has perhaps added to its repute:

> With margeran gentle,
>   The flower of goodlihood,
> Embroidered the mantle
>   Is of your maidenhood,

wrote Skelton, and Marjoram, if it is not quite up to the Tennysonian standard of amaranth and moly, has a distinctly incantatory ring. Miss Pratt points out that the plant is common near Dover, and hazards a guess that "Sweet Marjoram," the pass-word used between Lear and Edgar, was chosen by Shakespeare for this reason—a pleasant theory which I can claim to have evolved myself, in childhood, and quite independently of Miss Pratt; coming on the phrase in *Lear*, it seemed to me perfectly in order, for I, like Miss Pratt, knew that Marjoram was abundant on the Dover cliffs. "Village people," adds Miss Pratt, "often gather, during Autumn, large quantities of Marjoram, some of which is used while fresh for herb tea, while some is tied up in bunches, and hung to dry for winter service." Marjoram has also been used to flavour beer; and according to Culpepper, was good "against Pains and Torments in the Belly," and for taking away the marks of bruises. "The sweete marjeromes," says Parkinson, "are not only much used to please the outward senses in nosegaies, and in the windowes of houses, as also in swete powders, swete bags, and swete washing waters, but are also of much use in physicke, to comfort the outward members and parts of the bodie, and the inward also."

[1] *Flora Londiniensis.*

Many of the late summer flowers have, as I have remarked, an overblown and rather blowsy air; and none more so than the Evening Primrose, which adorns—or perhaps afflicts would be a better word—waste patches and roadsides in many districts. "It is found abundantly on the Lancashire coast," says Mrs. Lankester, "and covers several acres of ground near Woodbridge in Suffolk." It has, she adds, been "immortalized" by "the Suffolk poet Bernard Barton"; here is a sample from the immortal lines:

> Fair flower that shunn'st the glare of day
>   Yet lov'st to open, meekly bold,
> To evening's hues of sober grey,
>   Thy cup of paly gold,
>
> I love to watch, at silent eve,
>   Thy scatter'd blossoms' lonely light,
> And have my inmost heart receive
>   The influence of that sight . . .
>
> But still more animating far,
>   If meek religion's eye may trace,
> E'en in thy glimmering earth-torn star
>   The holier hopes of grace . . .

I confess that I do not share Bernard Barton's enthusiasm for the Evening Primrose, nor does it (alas) inspire me with any "hopes of grace." The roots, adds Mrs. Lankester, reverting rather abruptly to practical matters, are edible, "and were formerly taken after dinner to flavour wine, as olives are now; therefore the genuine name was changed from *Onagra*, the Ass Food, to *Oenothera*, the Wine-trap. We are not sure whether the change was necessary for such as need an incentive to imprudent potations."

I have mentioned a number of plants whose ancient repute in magic and medicine is hard to account for; but none is more baffling than the Vervain, *Verbena officinalis*. Whether the plant we know by this name is really the same as the classical Verbena, is open to doubt; but

the case in its favour seems at least as strong as any argument against
it, so one can only accept the tradition for what it is worth. It was held
sacred, according to Pliny, by the Druids of Gaul, and by the Romans
themselves; its repute as a magical herb survived through the dark
ages into mediæval times, and, in a diminished form, until considerably
later: "In our own country," says Anne Pratt, "the plant was called
Holy herb, and was connected with several superstitious usages. . . .
Even of late years the author has seen a piece of Vervain root tied
round the neck of a child as a charm to cure the ague, and was told
that the plant required to be attached to a white satin ribbon in order
to ensure its efficacy."

Gerarde recommends it for various complaints, especially "tertian
and quartaine fevers"—but, he adds, "you must observe mother
Bumbies[1] rules to take just so many knots or sprigs, and no more,
least it fall out so that it do you no good." About its magical virtues
he is more sceptical: "Many odde olde wives' fables are written of
Vervaine tending to witchcraft and Sorcerie, which you may reade
elsewhere, for I am not willing to trouble your eares with reporting
such trifles, as honest eares abhorre to heare." None the less, he adds—
following Pliny—"that if the dining roome be sprinckled with water
in which the herbe hath been steeped, the guests will be the merrier."
Culpepper also gives a long list of diseases in which Vervain was
effective: he mentions, among others, "Frenzy, Morphew, and
Freckles," and recommends it especially for "cold griefs" of the womb.

It is hard indeed to imagine how this insignificant plant acquired its
reputation: its spikes of tiny lavender flowers can scarcely, in themselves, have suggested magical virtues, to the Druids or anybody else.
Yet the magic was there, evidently; and there are innumerable
references to its uses in mediæval times. It was chiefly used as a protection *against* witchcraft: Aubrey, in his *Miscellanies*, quotes the following couplet:

> Vervain and Dill
> Hinders Witches from their will,

[1] Of this lady's qualifications I must confess to total ignorance.

and Scot, in *The Discovery of Witchcraft*, writes: "To be delivered from Witches . . . they hang in their Entries an hearbe called pentaphyllon, Cinquefole, also an Olive branch, also Frankincense, Myrrh, Valerian, Verven, Palme, Antirchmon, etc., also haythorne, otherwise White-thorn gathered on Maie daie." Scot adds that, "at the gathering of these magicall herbs, the *Credo* is necessarie to be said . . . and also the *Pater noster*, for that is not superstitious."

According to Gerarde, the Vervain was also known as "Iunos teares, Mercuries moist bloude, Holie herbe, and of some Pigeons grasse, or Columbine, bicause Pigeons are delighted to be amongst it, as also to eate thereof, as *Apuleius* writeth."

September

"THOSE who have dwelt or travelled in any of our hop counties, as Kent, Sussex, or Hereford, in the autumnal season, need not be reminded of the beauty of the hop-garden, or of its delicious fragrance. . . . It is a picturesque scene, too, when the tall plant, covered with its golden cones, is gathered by the hop-picker, and when we may see men, women, and little children, working beneath the blue sky at their employment, while the cradled infant sleeps the sounder from the soothing influence of the hops which hang over its head. The toil is not a wearisome one, and is lightened by the pleasant air and social intercourse, while often among those pickers may be found some-one who has come hither from the distant town to seek the long-lost health, and has found it here."

I have quoted this passage as a specimen, merely, of Miss Pratt's more lyrical flights. The diction, I admit, is not very distinguished; it is full of echoes of minor Victorian verse—"toil," "wearisome," "cradled infant"; yet I must confess that I rather enjoy such prose. Lenitive, slightly elegiac, eminently Victorian, it has a faintly pungent taste of its own, comparable to the aroma of one of those "herbal teas" which Miss Pratt herself so often recommends.

Hop-picking, nowadays, is hardly so "picturesque" as it was in Miss Pratt's day; I can remember in my own childhood the hordes of east-enders and gipsies descending upon the hop-gardens, the squalid huts in which they camped, the alien and rather frightening faces crowding to the village pub in the warm evenings. Nowadays, it is all much better organized and hygienic: there are special fast trains from London, aseptic "dormitories," Red Cross dispensaries, community sing-songs, etc., etc. Yet hop-picking remains a pleasant

E*

function, the nearest approach in this country to a genuine rural festival.

Miss Pratt's elegiac prose is well suited to these "aftermaths of soft September," days in which the long, calm decline of the year seems to prolong itself into a perpetual summer. The flowers of July linger along the hedge-sides, and on the foreshore, where one goes to bathe in the last hot afternoons, the Horned Poppy still flaunts its golden chalices. The woods are still bright with Willowherb and St. John's-wort; on the downs, Scabious and Felwort preserve an illusion of high summer, though the air is full of drifting thistle-down, and floating cobwebs fall gently, like the touch of a ghost, upon one's cheek.

It is on the downs, chiefly near the sea, that one will find one of the latest flowers of the year—a small orchid, inconspicuous but charming, the Lady's Tresses. Its flowers are arranged in a spiral spike, supposed to resemble a plait of hair: but the name, like so many orchid names, seems rather far-fetched and *voulu*. Not the least of the charms of Lady's Tresses is its scent, which resembles that of Lilies-of-the-valley; and the plant has the odd habit of producing its leaves independently of the flower. The root consists of a pair of parsnip-shaped tubers ("dead-men's fingers") the older of which produces the flower-spike; the leaves spring from the younger (next year's) tuber, and appear to belong to a separate plant.

Lady's Tresses is the only common member of a genus, *Spiranthes*, which has two other representatives in this country, both extremely rare. *Spiranthes æstivalis* used to be found in Jersey, in the New Forest, and in Wyre Forest, Worcestershire: it may survive in Jersey, but in England it is almost if not quite extinct: it is rumoured to linger on in one or two bogs in the New Forest, but I know more than one botanist who, in recent years, has searched its supposed haunts in vain. The other species, *Spiranthes Romanzoffiana*, occurs in the neighbour-hoods of Bantry Bay and Lough Neagh; elsewhere, it is to be found only in North America and Kamschatka.

But the true flower of September is the Meadow Saffron, often called Autumn Crocus: strictly speaking it is not a crocus at all, though it looks uncommonly like one. Like the Lady's Tresses, it produces its flowers and foliage separately: the leaves do not appear till the following spring, a fact which accounts for some of the odd names which have been applied to the plant. "Saffron," said Gerarde, "seedeth first, and fower months afterwards bringeth foorth flowers: and therefore the Latins thought this a fit name for it, *Filius ante Patrem*: and we accordingly may call it, the Sonne before the Father." Gerarde is not, in fact, quite correct in saying that the plant "seedeth first"; but the Meadow Saffron has the unusual habit of producing its seeds *below ground*: the "flower-stalk" is, in fact, a mere extension of the flower itself, a hollow tube through which the style, immensely prolonged, passes from the stigma down to the subterranean ovary. The seeds do not ripen until the spring, at the season when the leaves appear; hence the belief that they preceded the flower.

Meadow Saffron is also known as "Naked Boys"—a name which seems to me admirably descriptive; the generic name, *Colchicum*, is derived from Colchis, where the plant is said to be abundant. In France it is known as *Mort au Chien*: why it should be thought particularly harmful to dogs is not clear; one would have supposed that cattle would be its chief victims. Meadow Saffron is poisonous, but the drug colchicum is extracted from it: "The famous *Eau médicinale*," says Miss Pratt, "so praised for its cure of gout, is composed mainly of a tincture of this plant: and in Switzerland, where the ancient repute of its medicinal virtues remains in full power, the peasantry tie the flowers around the neck of sickly children as a restorative." Gerarde also recommends the roots of the Saffron for gout; and "the same," he says, "strengtheneth, nourisheth, and maketh good juice, increaseth sperme or naturall seede, and is also good to clense ulcers and rotten sores." It was to be used, however, with caution, and Gerarde adds that "the churlish working of that *Hermodactile*, or meade saffron, which is used in shops," can be corrected by "the powder of Ginger, long Pepper, Annise seede, or Commin seed, and a little Masticke."

If one had incautiously made a picnic lunch off wild Meadow Saffron, it was advisable to "drinke the milke of a cow, or els death presently ensueth."

Once, spending an autumn in Switzerland, I astonished my hostess by my evident delight at the meadows full of *colchiques*. "But they are very common," she said, "when I was in England I saw fields of them." Impossible, I said: I had never once found the Meadow Saffron wild in Britain. "But yes," she insisted, "I have seen many fields full of *colchiques*, when I stayed with my friends in the West of England." And, of course, the lady was right: in the West Country the Meadow Saffron is often abundant; but I had never been to the right places at the right time. To me, because I had never found it, the Meadow Saffron remained a rare English wild flower. It is, in fact, like the daffodil, distinctly local; I don't think one can find it anywhere east of Dorset, nowadays, and it seems always to have been chiefly a West Country plant. In Gerarde's day, it grew "in fat and fertill medowes, as about Vilford and Bathe, as also in the medowes neere to a small village in the West part of England called Shepton Mallet, in the medowes about Bristow, in Kingstroppe medow neere unto a water mill as you go from Northampton to Holmeby house upon the right hand of the way, and likewise in great plentie in Nobottle-woode, two miles from the saide town of Northampton, and many other places."

In the "language of flowers," Meadow Saffron signifies "My best days are past"—presumably for no better reason than that it flowers in the autumn. This at least seems a more reasonable interpretation than certain other examples in this odd and arbitrary *lingua franca*. Why should Valerian, for instance, signify "Rupture"? Or—more curious still—the Grass-leaved Goosefoot (*Chenopodium altissimum*) "I declare war against you"? "In some parts of Italy," says Robert Tyas, "the offering to any one of the stems or stalks of it is regarded as an insult." Nor do Goat's Rue ("Reason"), Fumitory ("Hatred"), or Mugwort ("Happiness") seem very felicitous emblems of the qualities attributed to them.

I have spoken of the hop-gardens, but not of the Wild Hop, which is common enough in the hedges, though said to be a "doubtful native."

> Hops, Reformation, Bays and Beer,
> Came into England all in one year,

runs the old rhyme—I quote one of many versions of it, none of which, I imagine, can claim to be historically accurate. Whenever it was introduced, the Hop seems to have established itself with considerable tenacity, not merely in the hop-gardens, but as a "wild" plant. Gerarde describes two distinct kinds—the wild and cultivated—and recommends them, not only as an ingredient in beer, but for "stoppings of the liver, the spleene and the kidneies," and to "purge the bloud from all filthines." He also recommends the young shoots as a "sallet," and very good they are, though personally I prefer them cooked, and eaten with melted butter, like asparagus. "The manifold vertues in Hops," Gerarde adds, "do manifestly argue the holsomnesse of Beere above Ale; for the Hops rather make it a Phisicall drinke to keep the body in health, then an ordinarie drinke for the quenching of our thirst." (The names "beer" and "ale," by the way, seem to have been reversed in our day: it is the non-bitter brew, known as "mild," which goes by the name of "beer," while the hop-flavoured "bitter" is called "ale"—this is the case, at any rate, in my part of the country.)

September, as I have already remarked, has few flowers of its own—plants, that is to say, which begin their flowering season during the month. For the botanist, it is an opportunity to catch up with any summer flowers which he may have missed; and I may as well follow his example, and mention a few which I myself have omitted from these pages.

I have not, for instance, had anything to say about that vast group of composite plants known loosely as *Hieracia* (there is nothing in the least hieratic about them): these include the genus *Hieracium*, and the allied genera *Leontodon*, *Picris*, *Crepis*, and *Hypochœris*. All these plants have yellow, dandelion-like flowers, and their combinations and permutations are more baffling than those (even) of the Marsh Orchids and the Wild Roses. One of the very common kinds—the Cat's-ear, *Hypochæris radicata*—is one of the prettiest, with lemon-yellow flowers which remain in bloom well into September. *Picris echioides*, the Bristly Ox-tongue, is a favourite of mine, too: it is easily distinguished by the curious, bristly involucres in which the flowers sit primly as though in a vase. The rest of these Hawkbits, Hawk's-beards, Cat's-ears and Ox-tongues must be left to the specialist.

I have not mentioned many of the Mint family (*Labiateæ*), either: not because I don't like them, but because their name (like that of the *Hieracia*) is legion. An autumn species, *Galeopsis ladanum*, the Red Hemp-nettle, is worth notice: it covers large areas in stubble fields with its bright, rose-pink, white-spotted flowers, and is rather local, though common enough in many places. It is not to be confused with the true Hemp-nettle, a much larger, coarser plant, found in the woods. Somewhat like the Red Hemp-nettle, though belonging to a different family, are the Louseworts, or Red-rattles: the small species is found in dry fields, the larger (*Pedicularis palustris*) in bogs and marshes. The marsh species is the handsomer of the two; better known than either is the Yellow-rattle, abundant in moist meadows. All these "rattles" are believed to be partly parasitic, and are viewed with dislike by farmers.

I am tempted to mention two other plants which may (if one is lucky enough) be found in September; but I do so with a slight sense of "cheating," for one is an alien, and the other so rare that very few (if any) living Englishmen have ever set eyes upon it. The Cyclamen (*Cyclamen hederifolium*) cannot claim British nationality, but is well-established in some districts, covering the ground in plantations with its tongues of pink flame:

> Dawn-rose,
> Sub-delighted, stone-engendered
> Cyclamens, young cyclamens
> Arching
> Waking, pricking their ears
> Like delicate very-young greyhound bitches

Half-yawning at the open, inexperienced
Vista of day,
Folding back their soundless, petalled ears.[1]

Lawrence is writing of Sicilian Cyclamens, and our own "English" plant is chiefly, I believe, a Mediterranean species. In southern Europe two kinds occur—one flowering in autumn, the other in spring.

Epipogon aphyllum is, I suppose, the rarest British plant; unlike the Cyclamen, it is a true native, but has been found (so far as I have been able to trace the records) only eight times in Britain—and usually only a single plant at a time. First discovered in 1854, near Tedstone Delamere, Hereford, it has turned up since then in one or two other counties. It is a saprophytic orchid, a leafless plant with a loose spike of pallid, yellowish flowers; its rarity is perhaps partly due to the fact that it is capable of vegetating for many years underground, throwing up a flower-spike only at long intervals. This habit of invisibility is a good protection, at any rate: were its appearances to become more frequent, it would stand little chance, one imagines, against the ravages of collectors. It appears to be nowhere very common, though it is said to be less rare in Sweden than elsewhere. One would have supposed that its scarcity would have protected it not only against the botanist but also against the herbalist; strange to relate, however, it has been recommended, by Gmelin, as a cure for epilepsy.

[1] D. H. Lawrence: *Birds, Beasts and Flowers.*

October

The green elm with the one great bough of gold
Lets leaves into the grass slip, one by one,—
The short hill grass, the mushrooms small, milk-white,
Harebell and scabious and tormentil,
That blackberry and gorse, in dew and sun,
Bow down to; and the wind travels too light
To shake the fallen birch leaves from the fern;
The gossamers wander at their own will.
At heavier steps than birds' the squirrels scold.
The rich scene has grown fresh again and new
As Spring and to the touch is not more cool
Than it is warm to the gaze . . . [1]

THE season is, in fact, a kind of second spring, yet as different as dusk is from dawn. The sun has the warmth of March, but is tempered by denser and damper airs. The late summer flowers linger on until the first frosts: some even survive them. In spring one watches for the first flowers; in autumn the process is reversed, one pursues the last survivors into sheltered crannies where the frost has not touched them, and derives a thrill from finding a summer—or even a spring—flower in October. Red Campion, for instance—a spring and early-summer flower, appearing in April or May, and lasting through June, the Campion should, by rights, be over by July; yet no plant is more persistent: one will find its pink buttons surviving in odd corners right up to Christmas-time. And as Thomas says, "Harebell and scabious and tormentil" last well into the autumn. October, however, has one flower of its own—apt to be overlooked, and not notably

[1] Edward Thomas: *October*.

144

beautiful; still, it is a flower, and this is its season for blooming. I mean, of course, the Ivy. Insects swarm to its rounded, greenish heads; the air round the Ivy-bush is loud with their buzzing. The Ivy's habit of flowering late was interpreted, in a more pious age, as a special act of providence: "Ivy berries," said Gilbert White, "afford a noble and providential supply for birds in winter and spring; for the first severe frost freezes and spoils all the haws, sometimes by the middle of November; ivy berries do not seem to freeze."

"Ivie as *Galen* saith, is compounded of contrarie faculties: for it hath a certaine binding, earthie and cold substance, and also a substance somewhat biting, which even the very taste doth shew to be hot. . . . The gum that is found upon the trunke or body of the old stocke of Ivie, killeth nits, and lice, and taketh away haire: it is of so hot a qualitie, as that it doth obscurely burne; it is as it were a certaine waterish liquor, congealed of those gummie drops. Thus farre *Galen*."

And thus far Gerarde, who had a rather poor opinion of Ivy. Culpepper, on the other hand, offers an imposing list of its virtues— it was good for "Bloody Flux, Jaundice, Spitting Blood, Worms, Drunkenness, Pestilence, Swoon and Dysury," among other complaints. "There seems," Culpepper remarks, "to be a very great Antipathy between Wine and Ivy; for if one have got a surfeit by drinking of wine, his speediest cure is to drink a Draught of the same wine wherein a Handful of Ivy leaves, being first bruised, have been boiled."

Proverbially tenacious, the Ivy will (almost literally) grow anywhere: the oddest habitat for it I have heard of is recorded by Anne Pratt, who tells us that "When last the coffin of Queen Catherine Parr was opened, a wreath of ivy was found entwining the temples of the royal corpse. A berry which had fallen there and taken root at the time of a previous exhumation, had silently, from day to day, woven itself into this green sepulchral coronal, and had wound about the brow where the rich golden hair had once clustered, and where noble thoughts had gathered, and our first Protestant Queen lay thus adorned in her lone resting-place."

Owing to its clinging habit, Ivy was often supposed to be parasitic; it is not, in fact, a parasite, but it is perfectly capable of killing a tree by the mere weight and tenacity of its overgrowth. One often sees, in the hedgerow, what appears to be an "Ivy tree," with thick trunk and branches; but it will be found that the trunk, in every case, belongs to another tree, long since fallen a victim to the embraces of its uninvited guest. Miss Pratt quotes, in this connection, a little poem by Calder Campbell:

> They blame me, they blame me,
>   Who understand me not;
> They say I suck the green bough's blood
>   Till all its leaflets rot:
>
> They say my roots beset the bark
>   Until 'tis little worth;
> 'Tis but my tendrils that cling there,
>   My roots are in the earth.

In Gilbert White's "Naturalists' Calendar"[1] there is an entry under this month which I find particularly pleasing:

"October 15–27: Gossamer fills the air."

When I first came upon it, this phrase set up a curious echo in my mind; it was some time before I traced it to Nashe's line: "Brightness falls from the air. . . ." The Naturalists' Calendar is full of fascinating references—I like the one for August 3rd–19th, for instance: "Oestrus bovis (whame or burrel fly) lays eggs on horses"; and (for August 20th) "Bulls make their shrill autumnal noise." An entry under June, on the other hand, might well cause dismay to those who know little of mycology: "Phallus impudicus appears." This, of course, is the Stinkhorn fungus, which may still be found now and throughout the autumn. One can only regard it, I think, as an obscene joke on the part of nature: one of those manifestations of a purely evil principle (the Giant Squid is another) which tend to shake one's faith (if any) in a beneficent providence. The Stinkhorn lives up to both its names:

[1] *Natural History of Selborne.*

147

it is a shameless and stinking object and (so far as I know) useless to man and beast.

Fungi, in October, are in their prime, and, with the autumn berries, compensate to some extent for the lack of flowers. As a nation, we possess some odd prejudices, and one of the oddest is our refusal to eat any fungus other than *Psalliota campestris*, the Field Mushroom. Many others are delicious, and only one is deadly—*Amanita phalloides* (even the Stinkhorn has not, so far as I know, been proved to be poisonous, though the mind boggles at the idea of anybody trying to eat it); yet we stick to our one and only "Mushroom," firmly convinced that all other fungi are "Toadstools," and, as such, lethal.

The Death Cap, *Amanita phalloides*, is a robust "toadstool" with an olive-brown cap and white gills, easily identified; other species besides this one may disagree with sensitive stomachs, especially *Amanita muscaria*, the scarlet, white-spotted species which, to most people, is the very archetype of a "deadly" fungus. It is not, in fact, deadly, but it is a powerful intoxicant, producing an appalling hang-over. None the less, the Fly Agaric (or Bug Agaric, as it is sometimes called) is used in Siberia on convivial occasions; the juice has the peculiar property of retaining its intoxicating principle when excreted in the urine, so that if one is not fussy about such matters, the party can be almost indefinitely prolonged.

Of the many edible species, one of my own favourites is the Parasol Mushroom, *Lepiota procera*. It is one of the bigger "toadstools," with a shaggy, scaly cap and white gills; umbrella-shaped at first, it becomes more or less flattened at a later stage, and I have seen specimens almost a foot across when mature—a single mushroom, in such cases, is enough for one person's meal. The flesh is very delicate, and should be cooked quickly—preferably in butter.

The yellow, funnel-shaped Chantarelle is common in some woods, and very good if stewed in milk. So are the two Blewits, *Tricholoma personatum* and *T. nudum*: the first has a purple tinge on the stem, the latter is violet-purple all over. *T. nudum*, the wood Blewit, has a tendency to be rather slimy when cooked, and is best used in pies and omelettes. The Horse Mushroom, very similar to the Field Mushroom but much larger, is perfectly edible, though rather coarse: it requires a lot of cooking. Puff-balls, viewed with horror by most people, are not only edible but delicious, especially the Giant Puff-ball, *Lycoperdon giganteum*. It should be peeled, cut into slices and fried.

The British prejudice against edible fungi seems to be of long standing, and Gerarde, for instance, has little to say in their favour: "Many wantons that dwell neere the sea," he writes, "and have fish at will, are very desirous for change of diet to feede upon the birds of the mountains; and such as dwell upon the hils or champion grounds, do long after sea fish; many that have plenty of both, doe hunger after the earthie excrescences, called mushrums: whereof some are very venemous and full of poison; others not so noisome; and neither of them very wholesome meate. . . ."

Many of the autumn berries, like the fungi, are more neglected than they deserve to be: few are considered edible, apart from the Blackberry and Bilberry, though this was not always the case. Hips, Haws, Elderberries, Sloes and a dozen others were once part of the housewife's provision; Elderberry wine may perhaps just survive, but few people nowadays use rose-hips for making those "pleasant meates and banketting dishes" referred to by Gerarde—"the making whereof" (he says) "I commit to the cunning Cooke, and the teeth to eate them in the rich man's mouth." Gerarde is willing enough, on other occasions, to supply recipes himself; but perhaps he thought the "conditing" of rose-hips a process too well-known to need description; or does one detect a certain irony in that reference to the rich man's teeth? Rose-hips in the raw are certainly tough and unappetizing; and their preparation must be tedious and laborious, for it is only the outer integument which is edible.

Loveliest of the hedgeside berries, though inedible, are those of the Spindle: glowing with a lurid purple, as though lit from within, they seem, at a distance, more like flowers than fruits; and when, in late autumn, the outer envelope splits open to reveal the orange seeds, the effect is intensified. Less spectacular, but very conspicuous, are the berries of the Wayfaring Tree, first scarlet, then black. Why this shrub should have received its name, I have never understood; it grows by waysides, certainly, but is to be found just as frequently in woods. "I know no traveller," said Parkinson, "doth take pleasure or profit by it more than by any other hedge tree"—a judgment with which I cannot but agree, though I would qualify it somewhat, for the Wayfaring Tree is pleasant enough, though less attractive than the Spindle.

Conspicuous, too, is the Black Bryony: its berries persist well after the long, trailing stems have withered, and look like drops of fresh blood spilt among the dead wood of the hedge. (The name Bryony, by the way, is a misnomer: it should really be applied only to the White Bryony, which belongs to a different family.) Hawthorn berries ("Haws") are, like rose-hips, a rather insipid fruit when eaten raw, though a pleasant jelly can be made of them. Nor have I ever succeeded in finding a sloe which was not intolerably sour, but I am told that when slightly overripe they are not unpleasant. They look, with their grape-like bloom, very appetizing, but seem to be useless except for making sloe-gin—an overrated drink, in any case.

The Wild Clematis or Traveller's Joy should perhaps have been mentioned in June, when it was in flower; it is, however, better known in its fruiting stage, as "Old Man's Beard." According to Gerarde, it is "called commonly *Viorna quasi vias ornans*, of decking and adorning waies and hedges, where people travell, and thereupon I have named it the Traveilers Ioie." Another old name for it is Virgin's Bower; though why virgins, in particular, should seek its shelter is not apparent, and the alternative name of Old Man's Beard can hardly be said to provide a clue.

With the first gales, the "fall" properly begins (it seems a pity, by the way, that we have lost this word to America: it is a far better and more expressive one than "autumn.") But there are years when the burnt ends of summer smoulder on well into November, and October goes out in a mild sunlit glory, with thistle-down and gossamer still floating on the still air, and the later trees hardly beginning to turn.

The rich scene has grown fresh again and new . . .

The year is fulfilled, the season is a kind of Silver Age lingering on, overripe and vulnerable, into the hivernal age of barbarism. Winter threatens from the north, but, one after another, the golden days prolong themselves, lapped in the false calm of a St. Martin's summer:

> . . . and now I might
> As happy be as earth is beautiful,
> Were I some other or with earth could turn
> In alternation of violet and rose,
> Harebell and snowdrop, at their season done,
> And gorse that has no time not to be gay.
> But if this be not happiness,—who knows?
> Some day I shall think this a happy day,
> And this mood by the name of melancholy
> Shall no more blackened and obscured be.[1]

[1] Edward Thomas: *October*.

November

In midnights of November
  When Dead Man's Fair is nigh,
And danger in the valley,
  And anger in the sky. . . .[1]

IT is the dead season, the ebb of the year: more deathly even than December, which at least looks forward to Christmas and the year's rebirth. All Souls' Night ushers in the month of the dead with the fires of Samhain; the Corn-God in the guise of Guy Fawkes is burnt again to rouse the sun's failing strength.

November, I think, is the only month without a single flower of its own; even October has the Ivy, and in December, as likely as not, one will find the Winter Heliotrope or even the Setterwort. The berries remain glorious; and in a mild year, the late-summer flowers still linger. It is the season when one appreciates, more even than in January, the "all-the-year-rounders" — Dandelion, Deadnettle, Shepherd's Purse. It would be interesting to keep a record of how many plants one could find actually in flower this month; I've never done so, but I would hazard a guess that I could, in my own district, and given an average season, gather the following (besides those already mentioned): Black Knapweed (*Centaurea nigra*), Groundsel, Primrose, Red Campion, Field Scabious, Ragwort, Nettle-leaved Bell-flower, Carline Thistle, Devil's-bit Scabious, Dog's Mercury, Annual Mercury, Black Nightshade, Yellow-horned Poppy (perhaps), Hedge Woundwort, Self-heal, Corn Poppy, Heartsease, Wall Pellitory, Petty Spurge, Sun Spurge, Wood Sage, Red Hempnettle,

[1] A. E. Housman: *Last Poems.*

Marjoram, Yellow Toadflax, Scarlet Pimpernel—and probably a good many more, but this would be quite a good bag for the deadest month.

Gilbert White's "Naturalists' Calendar" has two flower-entries for November: "Primrose flowers" (November 10th) and "Hepatica flowers" (November 30th). The Hepatica, alas, is a garden flower in this country; it has been so long cultivated, however, that it is surprising it has not naturalized itself; yet I have never seen it in any situation which could fairly be called "wild." . . . I like, too, White's entry for November 1st: "Bucks grunt"; surely the most admirably laconic sentence in English literature. Almost as admirable is his entry for November 22, 1768, in his *Meteorological Observations*: "A remarkable fall of the barometer all over the kingdom. At Selborne we had no wind, and not much rain; only vast, swagging, rock-like clouds, appeared at a distance."

> Th'imprison'd winds slumber within their caves
> Fast bound: the fickle vane, emblem of change,
> Wavers no more, long-settling to a point.
> All nature nodding seems compos'd; thick steams
> From land, from flood up-drawn, dimming the day,
> "Like a dark ceiling stand"; slow thro' the air
> Gossamer floats, or stretch'd from blade to blade
> The wavy net-work whitens all the field.
> Push'd by the weightier atmosphere, up springs
> The ponderous Mercury, from scale to scale
> Mounting, amidst the Torricellian tube.
> While high in air, and pois'd upon his wings
> Unseen, the soft, enamour'd wood-lark runs
> Thro' all his maze of melody;—the brake
> Loud with the blackbird's bolder note resounds. . . .
> For days, for weeks, prevails the placid calm.
> At length, some drops prelude a change: the sun
> With ray refracted bursts the parting gloom;
> When all the chequer'd sky is one bright glare.
> Mutters the wind at eve: th'horizon round
> With angry aspect scowls: down rush the showers,
> And float the delug'd paths, and miry fields.[1]

[1] Gilbert White: "Meteorological Observations" (*Natural History of Selborne*).

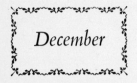

December

Ivy hath berys as black as any slo;
There come the owle, and ete hem as she goo:
Holy hath byrdys, a full fayre flok,
The nightingale, the poppyngy, the gayntyle lavyrok.

HOLLY and Mistletoe—I should have mentioned them, since this is a book about flowers, in the spring when they were in bloom; yet who thinks of the Holly and Mistletoe as having flowers at all?

The Holly, says Miss Pratt, "gives a peculiar feature to the landscape in winter; for at that season we have no native evergreen which is at all conspicuous, except this and the Ivy, and the masses of dark verdure yielded by these plants contrast beautifully with the naked outlines of the branches of the wood, as well as with the light tender green of the budding trees of spring."

I agree with Miss Pratt in admiring the "inscape" of the Holly—a black, living flame against the pale hedgerows. Its darkness has a more than nocturnal, a positively inspissated gloom; in the shrewd December wind, the leaves rattle with a peculiarly dry, hollow sound —Hardy (in *The Return of the Native*) calls it a "baritone buzz." Yet the wind seems scarcely to stir, visibly, the dark, solid mass of the tree, which remains static, an immobile pillar of darkness, among the storm-tossed boughs of ash and hazel.

The Holly was formerly called Holme, Hulver or Hulfere. Its wood, says Miss Pratt, "is still used for whip handles"; and a certain Dr. Rousseau, of Paris, "made very extensive experiments in the decoction of Holly, and discovered therein the existence of a hitherto unknown principle, called Ilicine, which appears to be of more service

155

in some cases than even Peruvian bark." Gerarde recommends a bird-lime "made of the bark hereof," which is "marvellous clammie," and "gleweth up all the intrailes, shutteth and draweth togither the guts and passages of the excrements, and by this means it bringeth distraction to man, not by any qualitie, but by his glewing substance."

The use of Holly for the "decking-up of houses" at Christmas is a comparatively modern custom; the Mistletoe, on the other hand, is so thickly incrusted with myth and legend that it is almost impossible to sort out the tangle. The "Golden Bough" itself was, no doubt, Mistletoe of a kind, though probably the true Virgilian shrub was a South European species whose leaves have a golden glint which is lacking in the northern plant. "The Druidae (for so they call their Divinours, Wise Men, and the State of their clergie) esteem nothing in the world more sacred than miselto, and the tree whereon it breedeth, so it be on the oke. . . . Certes to say, whatsoever they find growing upon that tree over and besides its own fruite, be it Miselto, or any thing else, they esteeme it as a gift sent from Heaven, as a sure signe that the God whom they serve giveth them to understand that he hath chosen that peculiar tree. And no marveile, for in verie deed Miselto is passing geason, and hard to be found on the oke."[1]

Mistletoe is, in fact, extremely rare upon oak trees, preferring apple and poplar. According to Vallancey,[2] it was "sacred to the Druids, because not only its berries, but its leaves also, grow in clusters of three united to one stock. The Christian Irish hold the Seamroy sacred in like manner, because of three leaves united to one stalk." Mistletoe, however (unlike the Shamrock), came under the Church's ban until comparatively recently. "I am of opinion," writes Brand, "although Gay mentions the MISLETOE among those evergreens that were *put up in Churches*, it never entered those sacred edifices but by mistake,

[1] Pliny: Trans. Philemon Holland.
[2] *Grammar of the Irish Language* (quoted by Brand, *Popular Antiquities*).

or ignorance of the sextons. . . . I have made many diligent enquiries after the truth of this. I learnt at Bath that it never came into Churches there. An old Sexton at Teddington in Middlesex informed me that some Mistletoe was once put up in the Church there, but was by the Clergyman immediately ordered to be taken away." Elsewhere, however, the plant was not only admitted into the Church, but was even held in special honour there: "the custom is still preserved in the North, and was lately at York: on the eve of Christmas Day they carry MISLETOE to the high Altar of the Cathedral and proclaim a public and universal liberty, pardon, and freedom to all sorts of inferior and even wicked people at the gates of the city, towards the four quarters of Heaven."[1]

The immense repute of the Mistletoe seems to me to be only partly explained by its parasitism, and by its general oddity; it is a curious fact (which I have pointed out already) that it is not, generally speaking, the obviously extraordinary plants which acquire such a reputation. Many of those used in magic or religious ritual—the Milkwort and the Vervain, for instance—are perfectly normal and uninteresting in appearance; whereas the really odd and outlandish species—the Broomrapes, for example, or Herb Paris, or the Bird's-nest Orchid—are more or less neglected. "The idea," writes Frazer, "that the life of the oak was in the mistletoe was probably suggested . . . by the observation that in winter the mistletoe growing on the oak remains green while the oak itself is leafless. . . . Primitive man might think that, like himself, the oak-spirit had sought to deposit his life in some safe place, and for this purpose had pitched on the mistletoe, which, being in a sense neither on earth nor in heaven, might be supposed to be fairly out of harm's way."[2]

The oddest thing about the mistletoe myths is their wide diffusion, and also their variety: the plant was associated not only with the priestly king of Nemi, but (in an entirely different connection) with Balder, and survives with an extraordinary tenacity in the folk-lore

---

[1] Stukely: *Medallic History of Carausias* (quoted by Brand).
[2] Frazer: *The Golden Bough* (abr. edition), p. 701.

of almost every European country—sometimes with a very particular
application:

> While the mistletoe bats on Errol's aik,
>   And that aik stands fast,
> The Hays shall flourish, and their good grey hawk
>   Shall nocht flinch before the blast.

> But when the root of the aik decays,
>   And the mistletoe dwines on its withered breast,
> The grass shall grow on Errol's hearth-stane,
>   And the corbie roup in the falcon's nest.[1]

Gilbert White, in his "Naturalists' Calendar," gives the following list
of wild plants as flowering in December: Gorse, *Helleborus fœtidus*
(Setterwort), Daisy, Wallflower, Mezereon and Snowdrop. One can
only suppose that the autumn of that year (somewhere between 1768
and 1793) was unusually mild—for none of these can be called true
flowers of December, unless one counts the Setterwort. Winter
Heliotrope, however, should be in bloom by Christmas or the New
Year—and so we are back where we started, the cycle is completed;
the last grey days of the year presage the awakening of January, with
the bulb-shoots pricking the garden earth, and the first snowdrops
springing in the plantation. Christmas is upon us, and the New Year,
that "festivity of Janus, which was spent in mummeries, stage-playes,
dancing, and such-like enterludes, wherein fidlers and others acted
lascivious effeminate parts, and went about their towns and cities in
women's apparrell. . . ."[2] But New Year's Day passes, for most of us
nowadays, innocently enough, and without any mummeries more
lascivious than the pantomime. At the end of the eighteenth century,
other and more ancient ceremonies still survived: "In the isle of
North Ronaldshay, there is a large stone, about nine or ten feet
high, and four broad, placed upright in a plain; but no tradition is
preserved concerning it, whether erected in memory of any signal

[1] Attrib. to Thomas the Rhymer (quoted by Frazer).
[2] Prynne: *Histrio-Mastix* (quoted by Brand).

event, or for the purpose of administering justice, or for religious worship. The writer of this has seen fifty of the inhabitants assembled there, on the first day of the year, and dancing with moonlight, with no other music than their own singing."[1]

[1] *Statistical Account of Scotland*, 1793 (quoted by Brand).

IN SESE VERTITUR ANNUS